ADVANCE PRAISE FOR

Organizing to Change a City

"The power of community organizing is changing the world. We only need to look at Libya, Egypt, and France to witness the profound change that occurs when communities act together for a worthy cause. *Organizing to Change a City* highlights one of the most significant forms of community change of our time. Rarely can a book compel us to act in ways that transform ourselves, and the cities we live in. Kitty Kelly Epstein weaves together a powerful narrative of community that confronts race, class, and urban politics head on."

> —Shawn Ginwright, Associate Professor in the Department of Africana Studies,
> San Francisco State University and Founder of Leadership Excellence

"This insightful book makes evident for all to see that politics determine economics. Kitty Kelly Epstein is a thoughtful scholar/practitioner, and breaks new ground with a disquieting analysis of global, national, and regional forces that surround Oakland and other cities in similar circumstances."

> —Melvin L. Musick, Adjunct Professor, Pepperdine University
> and Organizational Development Consultant

"Kitty Kelly Epstein shows that progressive politics are alive and well in the heart of our nation's remarkable yet troubled cities. As one of the nation's most diverse and dynamic medium-sized cities, Oakland emerges in her telling as a proving ground for new strategies of urban governance."

> —Robert Self, Professor of History at Brown University
> and author of *American Babylon*

Organizing
TO Change
A City

This book is part of the Peter Lang Education list.
Every volume is peer reviewed and meets
the highest quality standards for content and production.

PETER LANG
New York • Washington, D.C./Baltimore • Bern
Frankfurt • Berlin • Brussels • Vienna • Oxford

KITTY KELLY EPSTEIN
WITH KIMBERLY MAYFIELD LYNCH
AND J. DOUGLAS ALLEN-TAYLOR

Organizing TO Change A City

PETER LANG
New York • Washington, D.C./Baltimore • Bern
Frankfurt • Berlin • Brussels • Vienna • Oxford

Library of Congress Cataloging-in-Publication Data

Epstein, Kitty Kelly.
Organizing to change a city / Kitty Kelly Epstein;
with Kimberly Mayfield Lynch and J. Douglas Allen-Taylor.
p. cm.
Includes bibliographical references and index.
1. Protest movements—California—Oakland. 2. Occupy movement—
California—Oakland. 3. Political participation—California—Oakland.
4. Oakland (Calif.)—Economic policy. 5. Oakland (Calif.)—Ethnic relations.
I. Lynch, Kimberly Mayfield. II. Allen-Taylor, J. Douglas. III. Title.
HN18.3.E67 303.609794'66—dc23 2012010389
ISBN 978-1-4331-1598-1 (hardcover)
ISBN 978-1-4331-1597-4 (paperback)
ISBN 978-1-4539-0853-2 (e-book)

Bibliographic information published by **Die Deutsche Nationalbibliothek**.
Die Deutsche Nationalbibliothek lists this publication in the "Deutsche
Nationalbibliografie"; detailed bibliographic data is available
on the Internet at http://dnb.d-nb.de/.

Contents

Appendices

Acknowledgements and Appreciations

This book is about a movement–actually a number of interrelated movements. The number of people who have contributed to these movements is much larger than I or anyone else could ever name. I begin with personal appreciations and then attempt to list some of the thousands who have given their time and resources to these recent attempts at social progress.

I experience life as a gift and so I acknowledge first those who gave the gift, my mother, Edna Kelly, a steady and loving person and Andrew Kelly, a role model in stubbornly standing up for one's principles. I treasure my big sister, Robin, who I missed SO much when she left for college; my son, Jaron, who is my heart, and Ken, his wonderful and dedicated father And I acknowledge with love Ned and Danrey and Debbie and their fascinating offspring, Emma and Christina and Eric and Natalie and Kenny and and Ellie Kate. I acknowledge Fred Ellis, who has given to me his great humor, his deep knowledge and his enormous support and Dakiem Anderson Ellis, a brilliant young man. I also acknowledge those who have made internationalism real for me: Roberto Merces, Kim Porteus, Azalia Cruz, and Arega Yirda.

And those who struggle for change in the world owe to Ronald V. and Cynthia L Dellums a thank you which might have been best expressed by a woman at Berkeley Liberation Radio, when she spoke with despair about most politicians,

"'The only one I've ever known who wasn't like that was Ron Dellums. He said '"I don't have a magic answer; we have to create the answers together"' and he meant it.'"

Much credit to the many educators who have pursued social justice while inspiring their students: Audrey Cuff, Tamiquia Simon, Gina Hill, Diana Waters, Vincent Tolliver, Earl Crawford, Betty Olson Jones, Keith Brown, Cicely Day, Kyla Johnson, David Montes de Oca, Jerome Gourdine, Taslin Kimball, Mekael Johnson, Bill Dixon, and dozens of others. These colleagues have made their own unique contributions to the movement for educational justice: Karen Teel, Christine Sleeter; Laura Moran, Rachelle Rogers-Ard, Julie Henderson, Malcolm Bonner, Shawn Ginwright, Don "Four Arrows" Jacobs, Szabi Ishtai-Zee, Kathy Tiner, Margie Gonzalez, Lenneal Henderson, Nacole Predom, Emma Beal, Carla Sherrell, Jessica Ward, Monique Morris Nirali Jani, Chris Knaus, Paul Takagi, Jim Jarrett, Elnora Webb, Toni Cook, Sylvester Hodges, Jumokeh Hinton Hodge, Gary Yee, Rashidah Grinage, I acknowledge those people who first taught me what a movement was: Leonard Mudavanhu, Terry Collins, Rosy Wolf, Tembedza Chigovanyika, Jim and Arley Dann. And those with whom I first learned to teach, Patricia Williams Myrick, Bernard Stringer, and Betsy Schulz. These long-time activists laid the basis for Oakland's unique political movements existing in the world: Congresswoman Barbara Lee, Geoffrey Pete, Danny Glover; Rob McKay; Laniece Jones, Isaac Taggart; Bruce Buckalew; Bill Patterson, Jose Arredondo, the late John George, Gay Plair Cobb, Pam Drake; Gene Hazzard; Paul Cobb, Nabihah Shakir, Henry Rosales, Rashidah Grinage, Alona Clifton, Walter Riley, Lorna Brian Beveridge, Sandre Swanson, Keith Carson, Andre Spearman; Katy Nunez; Lynette Neidhardt; Robyn Hodges, Bob Blackburn, Denise Saddler, Dezi Woods Jones and a new generation of leaders like Marisol Lopez, Raquel Jimenez, Faye Stallings; Ze Segundo; Lailan Huen, Karina Nijera, Susan Curry, Nyeisha Dewitt; Kevin Cartwright; Chantal Reynolds; Kim Carter; Trina Barton; Erica Bridgeman, Corrina Gould, Faye Stallings, Marisol Nuno, Ben Wanzo, Corey Aguilar, Saleem Shakir, J.R. Valrey, Yaphet Santana; Carroll Fife; Henry Goh; and Jonathan Brumfeld.

And most deserving of acknowledgement for their contributions to Oakland are the amazing Task Force people who made "civic engagement" something more than the latest buzz word. They gave of their time to create a set of recommendations that speak to Oakland's values. Many of their recommendations have been implemented and all of them deserve to be: Larry Chang, Aziz Khatri. Chinyere Tutashinda, Kweli Tutashinda, Henry Hitz, the late Diane Howell, Melody Fuller, Angela Rowell, Hiba Sherry, Alternier Cook, Bob Schwartz, Marlene Hurd, Mark

Hall, Toni Cook. Steve Lowe. Walter Riley, Sylvester Hodges; David Nettles; Qa'id Aqeel; Randolph Belle, Ray Carlisle, Michael Lange, Darryl Weatherspoon; Ben Hazzard; Anne Huang; Linda Jolivet; MuJacinda Abcarian, Valerie Abad, Teresa Alexander, Robert Askew III, Gena Barsotti, Nadia M. Bishop, Dereca Blackmon, Stephanie Bocden, Rich Bolecar, Kareem Chadly, Jaron Epstein, Franklin Faust ,Glenda Frost, Gina Hill, Brenda McCuistion, Rev. Robert Lacy, Jr, LaTronda Lumpkins Trecinna Lankford Reyna Lett-Bell, Michael Lombardo, Marisol Lopez, Brenda McCuistion, Camillo Ochoa, Dorlista Reed Jason Sarley Deborah Singleton, Emily Villas, Helen Wu, Paul Kumar, Ingrid Lamirault, Raymond Lankford, Jen Lee, Dan Lindheim, Ethel Long Scott, Ophelia Long, Bertram Lubin, MD, Marty Lynch, Vanessa Moses, Ayodele Nzinga, Tonnesha Pace, Luella Penserga, Ralph Peterson, MD, Gayle Quinn, Yvette Radford, Debra Richardson, Glen Rosseli, Linda Rudolph, William Schlitz, Young Shinn, Ralph Silber, Jim Slaggert,, Ron Snyder, Barbara Staggers, MD, Frank Staggers, MD, Dong Suh, Melanie Sweeny, Minnie Swift Peter Szutu, Texeira, Richard Thomason, Asahara Tsehai, Gayle Wilson, Anne Williams, Pam Willow, Eileen Abrams, Jeff Baker, Reginald Borders, Colleen Brown, Sequonite Buggs, Retired (City of Oakland); Member, MacArthur Safety Team Margurite Fuller, Sally A. Keane, Don Link, Jason Victor Serinus,, Towanda (Hiba) Sherry, Dwight Stallings, Jr., Rashidah Grinage, Mary Vail, Nick Vigilante, Olu Oluwole Sr., Walter Riley, Grover Dye, Geoff Collins, Eric Sisneros, Glenda Deloney, Ericka Huggins, Dianna Jones, Celsa Sneed, Charles H. Turner, Nicole Lindahl, Troy Reagan, Margaret Richardson, Doris Mangrum, Roland Emmert, Rodney Brooks, Sara Bedford, Larry Benson, Alternier Cook, David Crosby, Charles Frost , Lorie Hill, Barbara Lafitte-Oluwole , Diana Lara, Josephine Lee, Stephanie Mann, Iris Merriouns. Stacy R. Perry, Charles Ransom ,Donald C. Smart, Darryl Stewart, Nanine Watson, Kim Hunter, Kimberly Price, Darlene Brooks, Ain Mulindwa , Terry Butler, Nicole Lee, Kathleen Jackson, Nina Horne, Dorlista Reed Chinyere Tutashinda Jim McWilliams Sidney Coulter, Nika St. Claire, Beatrice X, Langston Hill, Asha Lavert, Sandra Taylor, ,Aswan Boudreaux ,Lee Copenhagen, John Robinson, A. L. "Toni" Anderson, Qa'id Aqueel, Mark Bartlett, Bob Brauer, Stephen Clarke, Sam Cobbs, Stella Collins, Moyra Contreras ,Toni Cook, P. Lynne Corona , Jeff Dillon Naa Dodua, Milan Drake, Nicole Drake, Relena Ellis Ken Epstein, Janice Ewing, Amy Freeman, LaShaa Gatlin, Maryetta Golden, Ken Gordon, Hilda Fernandez Graves, Julie Hadnot, Pat Haggarty, Amy Halio Reygan E. Harmon, Susan Harmon, Phillip Harris Jennifer Henry Henry Hitz, Sylvester Hodges, Marlene Hurd, Debra Israel, Nirali Jani, Sofi Jiroh, Mekael Johnson, Ondrietta Johnson Barry Kim, June Ko-Dial, John Katz, , Mary King, Jerry Cauthen, Stuart Cohen,

Shirley Douglas, Cynthia Dorsey, Jennifer Jackson, Doug Johnson, Geoffrey Johnson Seth Kaplan, M, Nathan Landau, John Mack, Tom Manley, J. Pedersen, Aaron Priven, Robert Raburn, Michael Santee, Jesus Vargas, Mustafaa Abdul' Ali, David Bolanos, Bruce Cobbledick, Ann Hyde, Ken Katz, Gordon Piper, Jim Ratliff, Kerry Jo Ricketts-Ferris, Emily D. Rogers, Kemba Shakur, David Tucker, Susan Veit, MuJacinda Abcarian, Valerie Abad, Teresa Alexander, Robert Askew III, Gena Barsotti, Nadia M. Bishop, Dereca Blackmon, Stephanie Bocden, Rich Bolecar, Kareem Chadly, Jaron Epstein, Franklin Faust, Glenda Frost, Gina Hill, Brenda McCuistion, Rev. Robert Lacy, Jr, LaTronda Lumpkins, Trecinna Lankford, Reyna Lett-Bell, Michael Lombardo, Marisol Lopez, Brenda McCuistion, Camillo Ochoa, Dorlista Reed, Jason Sarley, Deborah Singleton, Emily Villas, Helen Wu, Bobbie Camacho, Gregory L. Chan, Miloanne Hecathorn, Randall Hughes, Michael J. Hunt, Jordan Pierce, Dwight Sterling Mary Weinstein, Lenore Weiss, Robert Bruce, Daphne Duverney, Chris Kattenburg, Lech Naumovich, Sylvia Chaney-Willimason, Cindy Thwaites-Smith, Susan Tubbesing, Harriet Wright, Kasey Brown, Martha Cline, Sarah Cohen, Peter Hauer Daria Kelly, Willow Liroff, Emily Rosenberg, Pam Smith, Kim Smith, Annalee Allen, Kim Anderson, Helen Bloch, Hattie Carwell, Linda Jolivet, Carolyn Mixon, Jenny Rockwell, Naomi Schiff, Jeffry Tibbetts, Jamie Turbak, the late Brad Walters, Winnie Anderson, William G. Pegg, Alton Jelks, Shirnell Smith, Joanna Adler, Ron Clark, Gay Plair Cobb, Mahlon Harmon, Barbara Harris, Helen Hutchison, Vance Johnson Alfonso Loera, Daniel Preciado, Wilson Riles, Jr., Angela Spell, Ruben Sundeen, Joel Tena, Margaret Cunningham, Horace Alexander, Mary Weinstein, Jonathan Dumas, Brian Beveridge, Margaretta Lin, Robin Freeman, Mujahid M. Abdullah, Rory Bakke, Belvie Rooks, Josh Bergstrom, Jose Cervantes, Gabriella Condie, Mercedes Corbell, Mercedes Corbell, Hugo Daley, Lori Dynes, Claire Greensfelder, Van Jones, Dr. Nazreen Kadir, Andy Katz, Navina Khanna, Ian Kim, Neil Mayer, PhD, Phillip McLeod, PhD, Payresh Patel, Linda Sanford, Victor Uno, Adam Weiss, Gwen Winter, Pamela Drake, David Glover, Dale Bartlett , Helane Carpenter, Denise Conley, Marcus W. Clark, Gillian Clarke, Joe Debro, Merlin Edwards, Howard Greenwich, Adam Gold ,Pronita Gupta, Teresa Harris, Hank (H.B) Jones, Joycie Mack, Andy Nelson, Charlene Overshown, Sarah Price, Gary Robinson, Art Taylor, Stephen Sanger, Charles Weber, Pam Weber, Maeve Elise Brown, Cathy Jackson, Christy Lefall Heidi Li, James Zahradka, Noah Zinner, Jonathan Dumas, Lorenzo Garcia, Geoffrey Pete, Deborah Barnes, Doug Bloch, Len Canty, Robyn Hodges, Jennifer Lin, Arvon Perteet, Carl Rice, Michael Steinback, Trina Barton, Solomon Belette, Wendall Chin, Janet Cox, Sandra Frost, Michael Gabriel, Susan Hayes-Smith, Evelyn Harris, Rebecca Holder, Angela

Johnson Abdul Luqman Liana Molina, Vanessa Moses, Katy Nunez-Adler, Maxine Oliver-Benson, Kenna Stormogipson, Bouapha Toommaly, Teresita Zaragoza, Virginia Sung, Catherine Tactaquin, Luz Buitrago, Larisa Casillas, Lillian Galedo, Gerald Lenoir, Michael Radding, Laura Rivas, Phillip Tou, Jesse Wolovoy, Kimberly Aceves, Peggy Moore, Susanne Borman, Lori Dynes, Terry Hill, Carmen Iniguez, Janet Jamerson, Al Schendan, Toni Smith,Donna Murphy, Andrea Turner, Ola Andrews, Pauline D. Brooks, Barbara Cheatham, Tracy Jensen, Reginal Lyes Charlene Overshown ,Jane Robinson, Anne Spanier, Penny Deleray, Taylor, Jeff Weiss, Gary Flaxman, Jean Parker, Bob Blackburn, Betty Olson-Jones, Chris Dobbins, Leon Glaster, Brandy Cowan, Valerie Lukaszewski, Cynthia Anderson, Quiona Jamison, Jumoke Hinton Hodge, Jason Willis, Chris Dobbins, Esther Lang, Eric Lewis, Dr. Ruth Love, Diana Lynch, Cynthia Mackey, Nancy Mackey, Michael Martin, Dr. Audrey McKnight, Heath Meadom, Paula Mitchell, Costlo Moore, Ruth Moore, David Nettles, Michael Pace, Osana Pulliam, LaJeana Reagan, Tanya Russell, Susan Schacher, Betsy Schulz, Sue Scott, Arlene Shmaeff, Rachel Sing, Darryl Weatherspoon, Elnora Webb, Beryl Weinwright, Brian Lavelle, Mark Williams, and many, many more. My sincere apologies to those who are not named. It is not that their contributions were any smaller, but that the number of active people in Oakland is so large that all of them can never receive the credit they deserve!

1

The Problem and Promise of Cities

"It could be worse. I could be a mayor"
President Barack Obama, Jan. 21, 2010

I live in a city because it's never boring. I learn a hundred new things every day, accidentally, just because of all the hustle and bustle. My city, like most others, has lost many of the industries that created it and has been hit hard by the latest financial crisis. It has foreclosures and violence and potholes. But I choose city life anyway and so do most other Americans (Lehrer 2010). We might expect that both the vibrancy and the despair of urban life would create more attempts at innovative and progressive leadership; yet in the past several decades, only small cities in the U.S. have elected self-defined "progressives" as mayor (Domhoff 2005).

But in 2006 and again in 2010, this larger city that I live in, with half a million residents and the greatest diversity in America, elected two successive self-proclaimed progressives as mayor, engaged 1000 residents in participatory policy-making, changed its electoral system, reduced the homicide rate by 40%, and implemented a number of egalitarian initiatives. In November 2011 the same city, a major site of the "Occupy" movement, saw a march of 20,000 people demonstrate its agreement with the Occupy message by shutting down the Oakland Port for a day. *Time* magazine editorialized that "Oakland has stolen Wall Street's mojo" (Motlach 2011).

Oakland, California, is the birthplace to some of the most famous formalized protests in modern America. It is a city that names public buildings after Huey Newton, Paul Robeson and Emiliano Zapata. Although its residents resent the tendency of mainstream media to treat it as either Crime Central or Pitiful Pearl, Oakland has learned to define itself in spite of the headlines. In the 90s we boldly advocated for African-influenced English with the school board's Ebonics resolution. In the 60s it was Oakland events that kicked off the Berkeley Free Speech movement when the owner of the *Oakland Tribune* complained to U.C. Berkeley officials that student pickets were protesting his discriminatory hiring policies. The Berkeley officials removed the student organizing tables; Mario Savio stood on top of a police car to address a crowd of thousands, and the 1960s Student Movement was born. Besides the protest politics represented by the Panthers and the student protestors, Oakland has put in place new electoral processes and participatory policy making.

This book tells the exciting story of defeating a political machine, involving a big part of the city in policy making, reducing its homicide rate, changing economic policy, moving to a new electoral system, and then defeating the machine again. The story is told from the perspective of an emerging activist leader, a wise journalist, and me. It begins with a community recruitment campaign to convince former Congressman Ron Dellums to run for mayor and ends with the election of the first Asian American woman mayor in the United States. The book aims to acknowledge the interplay of elections, protest, resident policy-making, and informal space-taking.

"The power of the people beat the power of the machine":

Recruiting a Mayor

Oakland is the type of place some people refer to as a "blues" city, the gritty boisterous working class cousin to more glamorous and refined, San Francisco. The beauty of Oakland is not found simply in fancy waterfronts, glamorous buildings and pristine parks, but rather in people and communities.

(Ginwright 2009, p. 26)

In the spring of 2005, a few of Oakland's African American leaders had quiet discussions about creating a mayoral choice who was in sync with their values and likely to win an election. In June, at a fund raiser for the community-based organization, OCCUR, Oakland Black Caucus Chair and political strategist Geoffrey Pete gave a dramatic speech about Oakland's need for a different mayoral candidate that ended with the words, "The person we need for mayor is our keynote speaker, our own statesman, former Congressman Ronald V. Dellums." There was a gasp and then an explosive chant of "Run, Ron, Run." During his own speech, Dellums didn't say "Yes," but he didn't say "No" either. The campaign to convince him began.

The significance of the event was immediately apparent. Dellums had been elected fourteen times to the U.S. Congress, beginning in 1970 when he unseated Vietnam War supporter Jeffrey Kohelan in the primary election to become the

Democratic candidate from Berkeley and Oakland. Dellums was the first African American elected to Congress from a mostly white district. In his own words Dellums arrived in Washington as the "bell-bottomed, Afro-topped, commie pinko from Berkeley." He played a pivotal role in founding the Congressional Black Caucus, ending the war in Vietnam, and releasing Nelson Mandela from prison in South Africa (Muwakkil 2006). Although he was always one of the most left-leaning members of the U.S. House of Representatives, he also became a revered colleague for such right-leaning Republicans as Newt Gingrich, who praised him for his courtesy and fair play. He was a homegrown statesman, a child of West Oakland, the neighborhood where the families of Oakland's sleeping car porters resided alongside soon-to-be sports stars like Bill Russell and Frank Robinson. The sleeping car porters developed the first African American union in the U.S., organized by Dellums' own uncle, C.L. Dellums, whose statue graces the modern Amtrak station.

A "Draft Dellums" group started meeting at 7:30 every Friday at the office of Geoffrey Pete in downtown Oakland. Mr Pete is one of the best political strategists in Oakland. It is not a business for him. He does not sell advice to random candidates. He is what the academic literature might call a "servant leader" who has watched and participated in a lifetime of change in Berkeley and Oakland and has an awe-inspiring ability to foresee both opportunities and challenges for marginalized people, particularly the black community.

A few rank-and-file trade unionists and a few more educators joined the effort. Soon there were offshoots, a "Latinos for Dellums" group consisting of thirty or forty attorneys, activists, and educators, including Katy Nunez-Adler, Annette Oropeza, Victor Ochoa, Jose Dorado, and German Martinez. And there was an "Asian/Pacific Islanders for Dellums," which included labor leader Josie Camacho, Health Services director Sherry Hiirota and environmental leader, Vivian Chang. We started a petition campaign to build the momentum that would bring the former congressman back into public life. Qa'id Aqeel and LeJeana Reagan and dozens of others petitioned on street corners, farmers markets, and the Art and Soul Festival. Lifelong activist Gene Hazzard enlisted his vast network. The petition ran in the *Oakland Post*, a newspaper read widely in the African American community, especially in the churches. Completed petitions were sent in with handwritten notes from seniors saying, "Please tell Mr. Dellums we need him to run."

We heard from Dellums' confidants that he knew about the petitions and was giving the whole thing a lot of thought. I ran into him at the Congressional Black Caucus and laughingly told him, "Your name is often on my lips."

"I know. I know" That and a worried look were his only response.

Dellums agreed that he would not announce a decision until we had a chance to present him with the petitions. By the time we had collected 8000 signatures, Dellums had agreed to a community meeting (Zamora 2007). With only a couple of days to prepare, we chose the auditorium of Laney Community College, notified the press, and arranged for a pre-meeting of petitioners with the congressman and his wife. Most who knew him, including most of his old congressional staff, predicted that he would not run. "He's a very private person," said one. "He's given enough. It will be too hard on him," said another. But a few residents who had been shaped by the same movements that shaped Dellums believed that he would. "He'll run," said one. "It's an opportunity to serve that is too big for him to turn down."

On the morning of October 7, 2006, thirty members of the Draft Dellums campaign and a few of Dellums' former congressional staff gathered in a small upstairs room at Laney College. Mr. and Mrs. Dellums appeared, holding hands and looking nervous.

No rock star has ever raised the emotions galvanized in that room. Reverently people appealed to him. A young Latina woman, holding her child, explained what it would mean for Oakland to be led on behalf of its ordinary residents. An Asian union leader made an equally heartfelt plea. A black minister told Dellums he had an obligation from God to run! Teary-eyed, Mr. and Mrs. Dellums asked for a few moments alone.

The thirty of us adjourned to the main auditorium to join the hundreds who had gathered there. Dellums began his speech like this, "I feel like a jazz musician. I don't know how this piece will end." And he took off in two directions at once, weaving together two opposing strands: a vision of Oakland as a model city and his personal fear of sacrificing his family again to the demands of public life. He explained that if he did become mayor, he and his wife would be partners in the effort because of her wisdom and the great collaboration they had developed. He later said that he had been prepared to say "No," but he saw people in the audience starting to cry. He ended his rousing oration with "If Ron Dellums running for Mayor gives you hope, then let's get on with it."

The campaign was unique for those of us who had grown used to candidate slugfests. Roberta Brooks, who had been part of Dellums' congressional staff, let us know immediately that Dellums did not do negative campaigning—under any circumstances. The campaign was unusually full of issues. The "Model City" was one of those, a concept that Oakland could be the model for urban policy making and resident engagement, "small enough to get your arms around; big enough to be significant." Andre Spearman, long-time labor leader and an active "Draft

Dellums" organizer, became the campaign manager. Los Angeles consultant Parke Skelton also supported the campaign.

Ron Dellums with Post News Group owner Paul Cobb.

Mayor and Cynthia Dellums with Sculptor Mario Quiodo. Bust of Frederick Douglass was a present to the Mayor.

Dellums was not supported by the Chamber of Commerce or the previous mayor, Jerry Brown. Yet he won the election without a run-off in a field of six candidates. His closest rival, Council member Ignacio de la Fuente, received 30%. Dellums' victory was citywide and included Latino, Asian, and white districts, as well as the African American neighborhoods of East and West Oakland. (This was before instant run-off voting in Oakland, meaning that he reached the 50% mark without any sort of run-off, either instant or traditional.)

Mary King, a former county supervisor and current transit official, said what many felt, "The power of the people beat the power of the machine" (Matier & Ross 2006). Geoffrey Pete said, "If you add in the votes that went to Nancy Nadel (a City Council member and philosophical ally of Dellums who ran third in the mayor's race), then you have a multiethnic coalition that must be reckoned with" (Matier & Ross 2006).

And the Dellums groundswell helped his former staffer, Sandre Swanson, to be elected to the State Assembly as the only African American from Northern California to hold a seat in the Assembly for many years (Matier & Ross 2006).

After Dellums was elected he asked me to work on education policy with him. I had never been inclined to undertake government work but Mayor Dellums was an unusual elected official: He had strong opinions; he did not mind if those around him also had strong opinions, and he did not care if they were sometimes different.

I have left a number of unanswered questions in this chapter. What do I mean by progressive? How does being "progressive" relate to addressing racial inequality? What is grassroots? I leave these and other questions to a later chapter, so that we can get on with the story.

The Organization and Purpose of the Book

In recent years only a few clearly identified "progressive" mayors have been elected, mostly in cities which are rather small and not very diverse. I am arguing that it is possible for a larger city to make change on behalf of the 99% through a combination of electoral innovation, resident policy making, movement organizing and strong leadership.

In making this argument the book explores the following issues:

1. Cities operate within a national reality and a local history that shape their current conditions. Developer interests often dominate; gentrification is either a feared future or a current reality; and the racial wealth gap is barely acknowledged.

2. A set of movements have challenged these realities in Oakland. These have included movements to recruit a mayor, alter the electoral system, employ local residents, regain control of the local school system, prevent the dominance of a developer-controlled machine, stop foreclosures, challenge the big banks, create land-use policy and involve the residents in significant policy making.

3. These movements confront internal problems as well as the more obvious external ones. Among these are the failure and apparent inability to support progressive elected leaders, in executive (as opposed to legislative) positions, after they take office; the lack of a communication system which can reach past the mainstream media, and a lack of understanding and action about race on the part of progressives.

4. In spite of these internal and external problems, Oakland has had many successes and its experiences are worth examining by other cities, activists and scholars.

I am not trying to represent the views of Mayor Dellums on his administration or his accomplishments. The text is informed by my own experience and my academic research. I have enormous respect for Mayor and Mrs. Dellums' willingness and ability to serve their community, but I have not discussed the book with them. I am sure there are many areas where our views would converge and some areas where they would differ. The same is true for everyone else mentioned in the book. They have their own ways of seeing what we are doing here; I am only trying to share my own.

I have discussed Oakland, the context, the recruitment campaign and the 2006 election in the first two chapters. In later chapters I discuss the national context and the history of the "growth coalitions" which, some have argued, run most cities. In Chapter 5, I describe in some detail the massive participatory policy-making endeavor called the "Task Force Process," which created some very important policy and practice for Oakland. Then I take up the specific changes in public safety, economic strategy, job-inducing policies, and education which flowed from the Dellums administration and the participatory process. Two later chapters are written by lifelong Oakland residents and social commentators, Kimberly Mayfield Lynch and J. Douglas Allen-Taylor. Kimberly weaves Oakland events into her own experience as an emerging citywide activist leader. Doug Allen-Taylor relates in fascinating detail how Oakland elected the first Asian woman mayor in the country and beat the more "mainstream" politician, who all but a few had predicted would win the 2010 election which followed Dellums' term. The book ends with a return to the problems of gentrification and the racial wealth gap, a description of some on-going campaigns and the "taking of space" so hugely embodied by the Occupy Oakland movement. I conclude with an analysis of tactical and strategic factors that will need development if big diverse cities are to see much social progress. The analysis is followed by extensive appendices that detail Oakland's efforts.

3

The National Context, the Racial Wealth Gap, and the History of Urban Governance

The U.S. ranks at the bottom of the industrialized world on most measures of equity and human development.

(Kloby 2004)

An interesting study by Michael Norton (2011), a Harvard economist, showed that U.S. residents would like a much more equitable distribution of wealth than that which actually exists. The figure on the next page shows in the first bar the actual distribution of wealth. The second bar shows the estimates made by Americans about the distribution of wealth, and the third bar shows what Americans consider to be the ideal distribution of wealth. Conclusion: U.S. residents want wealth to be MUCH more evenly divided than it actually is, and they think it is already more equally divided than it is.

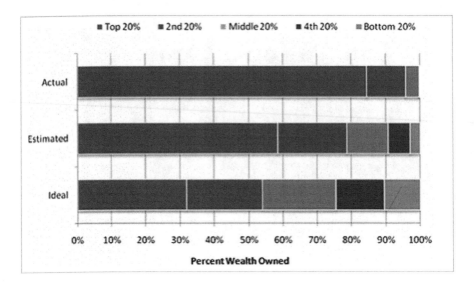

(Norton 2011)

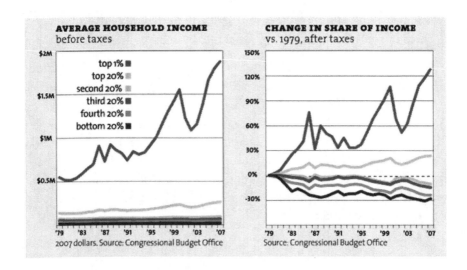

(Congressional Budget Office 2007)

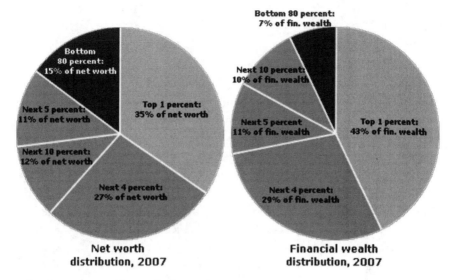

**Net worth
distribution, 2007**

**Financial wealth
distribution, 2007**

U.S. Compared to Other Countries

It is interesting to compare the U.S. with other industrialized countries on items such as income distribution. A comparison of fourteen industrialized countries found that the U.S. has a 16 to 1 ratio between the income share of the richest 10% of the population and the poorest 10%. Japan's ratio is 4.5 to 1. Norway's is 5 to 1. The only country that comes close to the U.S. in inequitable distribution is Australia with a 12.5 ratio between the richest and poorest tenths (Kloby 2004).

The Racial Wealth Gap

The racial wealth gap was 20 to 1 by 2011. The gap between the net assets of the median white family and the median black family grew from 10 to 1 in 2000 to 20 to 1 at the end of the decade. The wealth gap between white and Latino families is 18 to 1. This means that the black and Latino families who make up a large portion of most American cities do not have money to spend at neighborhood businesses; to pay in taxes for road repair; to pay for emergency health care, bus fare or movie tickets (Pew Research Center 2011).

There are some important points to make in regard to the significance of these figures. To begin with, wealth and income are not the same. Income is what comes into the household each year. Wealth refers to the total assets of the family: bank accounts, investments, businesses, value of the home (if you own one), stocks, everything of value. Although income is also unevenly distributed by race, the gap in wealth is much, much larger. The reason for the huge wealth gap lies in the history of the U.S.: slavery; sharecropping; redlining; the wars which took land from the Indians; the war which took large pieces of land from Mexico; immigration policy; standardized testing, which has always favored whites; the Homestead Act; and FHA policy, which allowed loans only on houses in "good" neighborhoods (and this did not include the segregated communities African Americans were forced to live in) (Pew Insight Center 2011).

Understanding the racial wealth gap requires an understanding of the difference between "mean" and "median." No one would be surprised to discover that the "mean" racial wealth gap is large. Most of the Rockefeller, Gates, and Buffett family members are white, and if we take an "average" by adding up all the white wealth and dividing by the number of whites, the number will be large because those white billionaires skew it in that direction, but this would not necessarily mean that the typical white family was much better off than the typical black family.

However, the median is not very much affected by the billionaires. If you want to understand that term, think of a hundred white families with their corresponding wealth as a set of dots drawn across a blackboard. Then create a hundred dots representing black and brown families and their corresponding wealth with the center (50th) dot at a point 20 times lower than the center (50th dot) in the line of white families.

Simply put, very, very few black and brown families have the level of wealth of MOST white families. One reason that most of us do not know this is because income differences are reported more frequently than wealth differences. Another reason could be that everyone is uncomfortable with the figure and does not talk about it.

It punctures a lot of bubbles for white progressives. We tend to think of most people, except for millionaires, as a general group of regular folk, and we might call that group either "working class" or "middle class." We know there are more Latino and African American families who are very poor, but we do not tend to think of whites as a separate and wealthier social class. In fact, however, a gap of TWENTY TIMES more net assets for whites puts us in a pretty different place from the rest of the country and makes it hard to argue that policies developed primarily with our input are going to be very "progressive" in the sense of economic equity.

The inequities are so stark that it has become mainstream to call for decreasing the overall gap between rich and poor, even though the proposed reforms rarely mention the racial wealth gap explicitly. Robert Reich, former labor secretary and currently a professor at U.C. Berkeley, has repeatedly called for increasing the taxes on the rich. He was joined in 2011 by billionaire Warren Buffett who revealed that his own secretary was taxed at a higher rate than he was. Yale professors Ackerman and Alstott propose a 2% annual wealth tax on those households with more than $ 7.2 million in net assets (Ackerman and Alstott 2011).

Most of the proposals about the racial wealth gap do not address it directly. For example, San Francisco's plan to open $50 college bank accounts for kindergartners is certainly a great concept, but the idea that it would come close to compensating for years of economic injustice is ridiculous and again puts the responsibility on the victims to create wealth from nothing. Policies like reparations, which would actually make a difference, cannot even get a hearing in Congress.

National Policies Fall on the Cities

Addressing a conference of mayors in 2010, President Obama acknowledged that he had had a tough week, and then joked, "It could be worse. I could be a mayor."

Ultimately the plight of the cities is bound up with national policies which have increased the differences in income and wealth. No one lives in a Capitol Hill office. We live on a block in a municipality whose local government unplugs the sewer so the neighborhood does not flood, stops the fire in the house next door, gives rabies shots to my neighbor's pets, and provides trash pick-up and security for the Christmas parade. If the residents have no personal assets, they will not be able to contribute to paying for those local services or to purchase at the small businesses in the neighborhood.

In addition to the impact of personal wealth inequality, the cities themselves have been defunded by the federal government. By the end of the Reagan administration, federal assistance to cities had been cut by 60%. Individual states have also defunded cities; California is one shining example (Schrag 2004).

The History and Power Dynamics of Cities

Those who study the power dynamics of the country have identified the owners of industry in a capitalist society as having great power to influence policy (Domhoff 2009). This power is based on the wealth they have accumulated by selling goods for more than the cost of producing them, leaving the captains of industry with the resources and the networks to demand policies that will create short-term and long-term benefit to their enterprises.

One of those who helped to popularize this perspective in the U.S., sociologist William Domhoff, argues that there is a somewhat different mechanism at work in the cities. Major national industrial capitalists are able to move their operations across the country and around the world in pursuit of cheaper labor and better markets. The real estate and development interests in any particular city, on the other hand, are rooted in a particular space and operate as a "growth coalition" attempting to increase their profits through enhancing the exchange value of their land. According to Domhoff, building on earlier work by Harvey Molotch, this growth coalition is made up of real estate interests, developers and City Hall insiders who work together in ways that increase the value of land on which the wealth of developers and real estate interests depend (Domhoff 2005).

As the country began to urbanize, these growth coalitions had little problem dominating the development of the cities. But with greater industrialization and immigration new political machines were formed, often based in ethnic communities with Democratic Party leanings. They relied on immigrant voters. In addition, the Socialist Party started organizing in 1901 and soon elected 79 socialist mayors across the country (Weinstein 1962).

The members of the original growth coalitions did not like these new power brokers, and they moved to create a series of "reforms" which took power away from the Democratic Party machines and the Socialists. Although some of the "reformers" were open about their motivations and said that "indiscriminate suffrage" was putting an "ignorant proletariat" in seats of power, most of them made the argument that the changes would create less partisan and more efficient government. Upon close inspection, however, the major impact of the "reforms" was to reduce participation in government.

These growth coalitions organized the National Municipal League and pursued implementation of the following measures.

1. They advocated off-year local elections when there were no presidential elections in order to produce lower turnouts, which meant a more conservative result.

2. They pursued a city-manager form of government so that voters could no longer choose the chief executive of the city.

3. They advocated non-partisan elections, so that candidates would have no party affiliation next to their names. This meant that the masses of the electorate had little basis for knowing the political affiliations and policies of the candidates.

4. The growth coalitions wanted citywide rather than neighborhood elections for City Council. Neighborhood leaders were no longer able to win elec-

tions, because they seldom had the money or the network to win citywide campaigns.

5. The growth coalitions advocated the elimination of salaries for City Council members. This reduced what the wealthy considered unnecessary and time-consuming public debate and meant that less wealthy individuals were no longer able to serve on City Councils.

The growth coalitions were successful in implementing these changes, all of which dramatically decreased the number of Democratic and Socialist elected officials in many cities and resulted in legislation on land-use policy, for example, which was beneficial to the growth coalitions. The ultimate result of these changes was to weaken city governments and the ability of regular voters to assert their power (Domhoff 2005). Thus, opposition to the interests of the growth coalition had to take the form of various protest movements, ranging from anti-redevelopment struggles in San Francisco to rent strikes and block parties.

What's Wrong with the Growth Coalition Anyway and What Is the Alternative?

Simply put, real estate interests, developers, and many City Council members are interested in raising the value of property in a city because this results in profit and potentially greater tax revenues. For the average non-affluent resident, however, it is the "use value" of a particular piece of property that matters, not its profit-making value.

When an absentee landlord's property increases in its exchange value, he is likely to raise rents, which means that his increase in "property values" is actually negative for the renter. Consider a piece of property next door to my rented flat that may be of great value to me if there is a park and a swing set for my kids; it may be of negative use value to me, however, if it is turned into a complex of expensive residences which increase parking problems and cause the new residents to demand more aggressive policing of my teen-age son and his friends.

The growth coalitions have posed "development" as a good thing for everyone. Their most common argument is that development produces jobs, which is often untrue. Building a residential building does cause temporary employment for construction workers, but they frequently do not live in the city, and the jobs end quickly. Building and staffing parks, recreation centers, senior centers, food and gardening co-ops provide longer-term employment, but they do not greatly enhance the land's exchange value and resultant profit-making of developers, and so they do not receive the same advocacy from these groups.

Progressive Strategy for a Just City

William Domhoff, an academic I have long admired, cites a number of cities which have had progressive governments. For example, Santa Cruz, his best example of a progressive city, has managed to prevent neighborhood encroachments and its progressive coalition has been very strategic in maintaining its authority in the city. However, the population of Santa Cruz is less than 2% African American. Given that the racial wealth gap is 20 to 1, this means that Santa Cruz is a city which does not need to devote much consideration to how to serve, employ, and enhance the lives of that group of people, which is, by and large, the most oppressed, marginalized, and impoverished in the U.S. The Santa Cruz population of Latinos is approximately 15%, less than half the 37% Latino population in the rest of California (Pew Hispanic Center), and Latinos are the other group suffering a large (18 to 1) wealth gap.

Domhoff also reports Santa Monica's many years of progressive government. Again, Santa Monica is not representative of the state with a population which is 3% African American and approximately 16% Latino. Domhoff notes that in many of the most progressive cities, the university students give progressive policy-makers the majority they need to attain power, but he cites Santa Monica as a good case of a city which has maintained progressive policy development even though it is not a university town.

Although the hard work of these cities in progressive policy development is admirable and their policy implementation is useful to study, further investigation and experimentation are needed to find and develop models for larger and more diverse cities.

4

Who Ran Oakland?:

The History of the First Machine

It is difficult for large and diverse cities to move forward on humane and innovative policy and practice even with majority support for the following reasons.

The growth coalition aims for the most profitable use of any individual piece of land, which is often high-end residential development. There is often a difference between what is profitable and what benefits the residents. This coincides with the desire of many white and relatively affluent individuals to move into the city, where theaters, restaurants, and other interesting urban amenities exist. Such developments do not generally provide any clear benefit to most of the current residents. They cannot afford to live in the new residences; they cannot afford the restaurants built to service the new residents; and more aggressive policing of the current less affluent residents often accompanies the newcomers.

Attempts at remediating the racial wealth gap (and the more general concentration of wealth at the top) through tax policy have been cut off by conservative organizing at the state and federal level. I urge readers to spend some time perusing three websites which make clear how dramatically important racial wealth gap issues have become:

The Insight Center: http://www.insightcced.org;
United for a Fair Economy: http://www.faireconomy.org and

Who Rules America? http://sociology.ucsc.edu/whorulesamerica/power/wealth. html

Education is posed as the answer to the problems of cities and the individuals within them. While education is important to a joyful and productive life, it does not, by itself, create jobs, produce reasonable banking regulation, reduce the wealth gap, or prevent the financial meltdown, which destroyed the small savings of many families (Epstein 2012).

The residents do not generally have easy access to clear information on such complex issues as the relationship between land use and the availability of jobs. They are disempowered by the lack of information which would allow them to be more demanding of elected officials. Few people study these subjects in school, and neither TV news nor city newspapers are particularly educative on these topics (Bagdikian 2004; Baker 2007; Media Access Project 2011).

Finally, constituencies which may vote together in national elections are often fractured locally. White progressives and other communities are often talking past each other. Like other big diverse cities Oakland has progressive constituencies, but it had not, until recently, moved forward with much progressive local policy making. Oakland did pass a path-breaking community policing initiative in the 1990s which explicitly required 57 problem officers, one per beat, to take direction from the residents in solving community-identified problems before they became major public safety issues. Oakland also initiated Measure Y, which combined violence-prevention with community policing. Problems with implementation of these attempts will be discussed in a later chapter.

On the longer list of issues which might create jobs, help small businesses, and create affordable housing, the council often seemed unable to act. There was not an effective land use policy, for example, and this meant high-end residential developers could build where they wanted, pushing out job-producing businesses. Jerry Brown as mayor actively and successfully resisted any policy that would reduce the flexibility of residential developers to build where they wished. There were various discussions about inclusionary zoning, but no legislation was developed. Local hire had become a policy, but it was gutted by administrative intervention, and no one really acted to make it work.

The council did not resist state takeover of the school district, nor did it act to return local control of the schools after the state did take over.

In spite of intense organizing the council did not pass an "inclusionary zoning policy" considered by many groups to be a pivotal part of creating affordable housing.

I could perhaps best summarize the policy making as a schizophrenic battle between two theories: the idea that Oakland needed to serve its existing residents with responsive local policy making, sensitive policing, and locally oriented job creation as opposed to the idea that Oakland needed the disposable income and business taxes that could only be produced by new, more affluent residents and unfettered construction projects. The most powerful local politicians of the era between 1995 and 2005 were Jerry Brown and Don Perata. (Barbara Lee was locally elected but served in a national seat.) Both weighed heavily on the latter side of that policy battle. Brown's most important initiative was downtown residential development for 10,000 people, most of whom were not expected to be Oakland's current residents, since few of those would be able to afford the new developments. Perata pushed for state control of the school district, a position which obviously took power away from local residents.

I believe that there have been three reasons for the schizophrenic policy actions I have described. The most important is certainly the influence of the growth coalition. Real estate and developer interests spend enormous amounts of staff time and money to pursue both policies and individual regulatory decisions which favor them; at one point there were five members of the City Council who could be counted on to regularly follow the lead of Don Perata—the "Peratistas"—and Perata was certainly the standard bearer for the growth coalition. (See chapter 13 for details).

Another reason that no clear justice-oriented agenda has emerged is the residual effects of the governance changes imposed by the growth coalition during the early part of the twentieth century. Prior to the mid-1990s Oakland had a council-manager form of government with a weak mayor. Mayoral elections took place in June of the gubernatorial election year when there are far fewer voters than in November. The past decade has seen the introduction of both a strong(er) mayor and ranked-choice voting. Both changes have already made a difference in the mayoral elections and may soon have the same effect at the City Council level. And the policy inertia on some issues was pushed aside because impetus was created by the task force recommendations.

The Political Development of Oakland: A Historic Poster Child for Unrepresentative Northern Governments

In the 1911 city elections in Oakland the Socialist Party received 9,837 votes compared to 11,732 votes for the other guys. The result frightened Oakland business. They also did not like the fact that much of Oakland politics was governed by people associated with Mike Kelly, a Catholic who served as Alameda County treasurer and later county tax collector. He was opposed by "good government" organizations like the Alameda County Organization, which issued a leaflet in 1918 accusing the Kelly alliance of "obtaining support from liquor interests and gambling joints." Opposition to Kelly was enhanced by Protestant middle-class prejudice against poor people and Catholics and sentiment in favor of prohibition. The political factions associated with Mike Kelly tended to be located in the older areas of West Oakland; the middle-class organizing tended to be located in the newer sections of recently incorporated East Oakland (Rhomberg 1998). Business took action with special committees of the Oakland Chamber of Commerce to draw up a new city charter. The new charter had significant benefits for business. The commission form of government which it established was less expensive, leaving more money to aid local business interests, and it removed party labels from the ballot, which greatly weakened the Socialist Party vote (Hayes 1972, p. 12).

However, a second charter reform was, according to political scientist Edward Hayes, even more beneficial to business. The council-manager form of government adopted in 1931 "augmented the power of business over city policy generally and of the *Tribune* over political elections" (Hayes 1972, p. 13). One city manager held the job from 1933 to 1954 and was himself the vice-president of an Oakland bank. The charter also established the semi-autonomous Port Commission, whose directors were, until recently, almost entirely businessmen.

The Racial Climate of Oakland in the 1920s

The racial climate of the city can perhaps be best illustrated by the fact that the Ku Klux Klan had opened a headquarters in downtown Oakland in August 1921, and in May of 1922, 1,500 men in white robes gathered in the Oakland hills to burn a fiery cross behind an American flag in an initiation ceremony for 500 new KKK recruits (Rhomberg 1998). In the 1923 election Grand Cyclops Leon Francis won 18% of the vote in a crowded field of school board candidates. Contrary to traditional interpretations of 1920s Klan activity, these Klansmen did not represent marginal groups. Oakland Klansmen included Protestant churchmen, members of the Oakland fire department, the son of a congressman, professionals, and small businessmen. Earl Warren, who was a district attorney in 1930 began pursuing a case against Klansman Sheriff Becker. Says researcher Chris Rhomberg, "Even at this time, Klan legitimacy in Oakland was high enough that Warren feared that Klan members on the Alameda County Grand Jury would refuse to indict fellow Klansmen" (Rhomberg 1998, p. 5).

By the end of the 1930s J.R. Knowland had consolidated a newspaper-centered coalition whose influence ran through every facet of public life. He was a bank director and a corporate director and his son, William Knowland, won a seat in the U.S. Senate in 1946 (Hayes 1972, p. 15). The Republican Party maintained a clear majority on the council throughout the New Deal: poor people received little relief; and the council was hostile to the labor organizing of the Council of Industrial Workers.

By the end of World War II, there was enormous labor dissatisfaction. In 1946 the Eastbay Retail Clerks attempted to organize Kahn's Department Store. At 7:30 a.m., December 1, police in 12 radio cars and 15 motorcycles escorted the first "scab" (non-union) truck into Kahn's to make its delivery. The AFL labor leaders called for a general strike. Council members spoke against the strike and so did the city manager, John Hassler; 1200 employers and businessmen then met in Oakland Auditorium to give Hassler a "vote of confidence."

This behavior on the part of business and city government led to a revolt by all sections of the labor movement. Railroad, AFL-CIO unions, and construction trades united to put up a slate of five candidates. The *Tribune* called the labor candidates "left wing communists" and editorialized against them daily, but the five labor candidates organized intensively. One tactic was a giant torchlight parade in which "the Negro Labor Committee" used a large float which showed AFL and CIO pallbearers lowering a casket into the ground. The casket was labeled "The Machine." On the side of the float was the slogan, "Let's finish the job—take the power out of the Tower" (referring to the *Tribune* Tower owned by the Knowland family). Their platform included rent control, school bonds, overhaul of the public health service, and other issues.

Despite the red-baiting and the extensive propaganda, four of the five labor candidates were elected, resulting in a Council divided 5–4 in favor of the old "machine." The corporate-political machine was able to maintain its power through the '50s and '60s. The first black City Council member was not seated until 1970, and the first black mayor, Lionel Wilson, was elected in 1977. Writing in 1970, Edward Hayes concludes that even strong labor and African American organizing had not changed the essential system which was established with the creation of the non-partisan ballot in 1911, the at-large elections in 1933, and the political influence of the *Tribune*. "The result is a system of mobilized bias. The basic politics of the city toward subordinate groups in the city, the moderate use of the injunction again labor, and the unlimited use of the police to control the flatlands go on unchecked while the city manager is dependent on an almost entirely white, business-oriented city council" (Hayes 1970, p. 190).

The Dellums Difference

By the time Dellums ran for office in 2006 the city had moved away from some of the 1920s governance policies driven by the growth coalition, but the changes were incomplete. Oakland's move to a strong mayor, for example, made the mayor the chief executive officer but accorded him a salary considerably less than that of the city administrator. Council members were paid and elected by district, but elections were still held in June, a time of lower turn-out.

Dellums did not believe in "negative campaigning." So, in his 2006 campaign he rarely critiqued either former mayors or current candidates by name. However, his election speeches asserted a progressive populism.

He did not explicitly refer to gentrification, but at a variety of campaign dinners and debates, he made such remarks as, "We don't want to become a bedroom community for San Francisco," and "We need to zone the city so that there is a predictable basis for job-producing businesses to locate here." And he addressed crime, not by blaming the residents, but by taking on the organization of the police department: "We need to change the policies by which our police have been scheduled to work on Monday afternoon when there is no crime, instead of Saturday evening when they are needed" (in reference to the stranglehold of the Police Officers Association on hours and overtime). He also said, "I'm seventy years old; this is not a career move. So I'm too old to be intimidated." (This was interpreted as a reference to the Police Officers Association's tendency to reward those who voted for their unprecedented contracts with hefty campaign contributions.)

Dellums was a veteran of the movements of the 1960s. More intense than his belief in any particular policy was his belief in people's participation. "There is wisdom and brilliance in this community," he said, "and I want to tap into this brilliance to make policy." "Oakland is large enough to be significant and small enough to get your arms around." And with some vehemence he would say to young people, "I'm tired of singing 'We shall overcome.' You need to come to the meeting, get yourself a roll, bang down your coffee cup and say, 'I'm here. Now let's talk.'"

His personal history as a youthful resident of West Oakland gave him lots of opinions about other important subjects like education: "Teachers need to live in the community, so that they are part of the lives of their students' families" and "We have the elegant idea of employing youth, ending poverty and saving the planet through one common strategy." This strategy came to be called the "Green Job Corps."

He wondered along with his audiences: "How can we have a safe city when hundreds of people return to our community from prison with $200, no job, and no services?"

It was clear throughout the campaign that Dellums would be able to use his extensive national contacts to generate more federal and state money than the typical mayor. While in Congress, he had succeeded in convincing the Clinton administration to spend millions on dredging the Port of Oakland and had, remarkably, been able to situate a federal building in downtown Oakland although one already existed right across the Bay in San Francisco. In addition, he would be able to utilize some of the limited "strong mayor" powers which Jerry Brown had been able to push through during his first mayoral term.

And most important perhaps, in the long run, Dellums, along with his community-minded wife, Cynthia, developed the elegant idea of community task forces which would "tap into the wisdom and brilliance" he mentioned in his campaign speeches (Heredia 2006). That process is the subject of the next chapter.

5

Participatory Action on a Grand Scale:

A Thousand Residents Make Policy

The task force process is the best social networking experiment ever devised.

Steve Lowe, West Oakland businessperson

Task force members get organized in the Council chambers of City Hall

Conveners of the education task forces make plans

Other mayors have had task forces. These were different. Eight hundred residents in 41 unpaid groups met all over downtown Oakland and decided on things like local hiring policy and land use policy. (Later more task forces of several hundred more individuals took up entertainment; sexually exploited minors; and city financing.) Every task force was diverse in ethnicity, income, age, and neighborhood of origin. "Notable" people did not receive either a special invitation or a special role. Everyone was equal.

The process was uniquely constructed to be workable for ordinary people. Each group was framed by a question. Therefore, the groups did not spend weeks debating exactly what issues to pursue. Instead of the general topic of "better schools," one education task force was asked a specific question such as, "How can Oakland ensure that there are enough effective, permanent, diverse teachers for all Oakland youngsters?" Another task force was asked, "How can the Dellums Administration assist the Oakland Unified School District in reclaiming local control from the State of California?" and another "How can the middle and high schools insure effective, exciting education and reduce the number of young people who do not graduate?" Eight education groups were examining different questions.

The nine economic development groups addressed a similar range of questions: "What relationship between the City of Oakland and the Port will produce maximum benefit to the residents?" And "What policies will protect the health and environment of Oakland residents, while fully developing the economic potential of the Port?" were the questions posed to the Port task force. The planning and land use task force was asked, "How can planning, zoning, and land use policies most enhance the lives of Oakland residents?"

A little magic and a lot of thought constructed a process which could accommodate the hundreds of enthusiastic volunteers with no budget and no paid staff. The National Community Development Institute led by Omowale Satterwhite agreed to help us think it through and get organized.

When we dreamed up 60 task force topics, even Omowale, also a dreamer, suggested that we reduce the number. He laughed when our consolidation could only get us down to 41, but he helped us anyway. Omowale lent his staff for the planning and personally participated in most of the participant orientations, bringing energy and a sense of movement history to the project. VaShone Huff and Diane Boyd worked to get things organized. Non-profit organizations like the Private Industry Council and the Health Department loaned us office space so that all groups could meet within a few blocks of each other in downtown Oakland.

We limited the number of task force sessions to six, so that those with low tolerance for long-term commitments were willing to participate. Everyone who volunteered was accepted, whatever their individual politics or personalities. Again, there were many critics who considered this completely unworkable and who thought that the task forces would be torn apart by "difficult personalities." It didn't happen. The 70 conveners of 41 individual task forces managed the meetings, gave everyone a chance to talk, and somehow no one ended up seeming "difficult."

The "conveners" were all regular residents with a bit of knowledge on the topic. All conveners were required to attend a workshop on a set of processes designed to make full participation just as likely for the non-affluent as for those with more money and flexibility. So, for example, conveners asked participants about their need for transportation or child care at the first session, and many people gave each other rides. And conveners were asked to have people raise their hands, a process which actually ensures more democracy and participation, because shy people are more likely to talk if they are recognized. They were asked to use phone calls and hard copies to communicate in addition to the internet, because the bus drivers and custodians who participated did not spend their days on a computer. (See appendices for process guidelines.)

Each participant was required to attend an orientation. Everyone was promised that there would only be six sessions, so they did not have to feel, as they might with other groups, that a task force could end up being a life sentence

Many skeptics, including some Dellums supporters, predicted assertively that the process could not work. They argued that there were too many groups, that unpaid volunteers could not manage them, that most would stop meeting, and that they would not be able to agree on anything.

One of the best ideas we had was asking people to "take off their labels" within the task force process and operate as individuals. We acknowledged, of course, that many people had employers or organizational affiliations that wanted a voice, but we did not want the task forces to break down into some sort of negotiation or debate between different organized groups. We were remarkably successful in this.

The skeptics were wrong. Every one of the 41 groups met for its full six sessions. Each group produced its complete set of recommendations and a binder of materials to back them up. And most significant perhaps, their recommendations rang with the sense of representing Oakland—real people with real ideas about what their city needed (Heredia 2007d).

The Results

The Movement

The most important result may have been the sense that there was a movement engaged in policy making. The mayor read all the hundreds of proposals. He sat around the big oval table in the mayor's conference room with the groups of workers and unemployed and teenagers and elderly and renowned physicians and computer geeks who made up the task force leaders so that he could hear their recommendations and the logic of their approaches. Dellums had a long-term knowledge of urban policy-making, having first served as a Berkeley council member and then as chair of the District of Columbia Committee in the U.S. Congress (Dellums & Halterman 2000). I have never met anyone in public life so willing to listen attentively for hours to what ordinary residents had to suggest. I believe he saw this process as the most important reason for being mayor.

Cynthia Dellums was a constant advocate for the task forces and their recommendations. She had agreed to her husband's recruitment as mayor because she saw it as an act of community service. She was therefore determined that the community voice would be strong within the administration. She played the same role in planning the inauguration of the mayor, insisting that there be events in every ethnic community and that every Oaklander who wanted to attend should be invited.

Kimberly Mayfield Lynch, in Chapter 11, expresses the opinions of many, "We, the people of Oakland, reclaimed City Hall for ourselves, made it our own and refuse to give it back."

The Implementation

The recommendations were implemented in several ways. In some cases the mayor simply declared that he was implementing a recommendation (the creation of a public safety director) or another public body implemented them. For example, when the education task forces presented their recommendations to the school board, the board members were so enthusiastic they asked the state administrator to implement all of the recommendations, something she tried pretty hard to do. In some cases, a City Council member or other elected official took up a particular recommendation and worked on it. Council member Brunner had wanted a business assistance center for years, and she saw the small business task force recommendation as a way to push it forward.

In other cases, city staffers saw a particular recommendation as a green light to move forward on some sensible idea, like using a community-organizing approach to resolve long-standing neighborhood problems (Heredia 2007a). Sometimes a task force leader took a recommendation in hand and began organizing the coalition that could make it happen. Industrial land-use policy was such a case and is discussed in Chapter 7.

Some recommendations were not implemented. Some required City Council action to set the policy. The City Council set up a housing task force, for example, and used the community task force recommendations as a springboard even though, in the end, they did not implement a new policy. In other cases, the recommendation would have been expensive. The task force on LGBT issues recommended a human rights commission, but council members concluded they could not afford the staffing costs.

Other recommendations did not happen because a four-year mayoral term is a short time. Many are still being pursued and the new mayor has blessed some of them. Some of those are discussed in later chapters.

A New Cohesion

West Oakland small businessman, activist, and general good guy Steve Lowe says, "The task force process is the best social networking experiment ever devised." Hundreds of people have networks of trust and assistance they did not have before, and they use these to move their programmatic agendas.

Implications for Other Cities

1. It is possible to carry out a participatory policy-making process without a lot of money. We were not tempted to hire high-priced, disconnected "consultants" because we could not afford them. The best "conveners" or chairs were egalitarian people who believed that everyone had something to offer and who did not insist on doing all the talking or using bureaucratic or overly technical vocabulary.
2. Communities of color need to dominate much of the process—acting as a majority of the group leaders, shaping the topics, interpreting the conclusions—if this process is to create a more just city.
3. Many of the materials in the appendices are relevant to other cities. The sample questions we used to frame the groups could be useful. Some sort of working agreements and training for conveners are needed. The website of the Oakland Alliance of Community Partnerships (www.oacp.net) summarizes all the Oakland recommendations.
4. Cities need to figure out a combination of structure and democracy which feels both efficient and inclusive. We found selecting conveners, creating the questions, limiting the number of sessions, and creating explicit processes ahead of time to be critical parts of mass engagement. It is NOT democratic to waste the time of busy people when minor organizational details could be figured out ahead of time.

6

Homicide Rate Drops 40%:

How a Progressive Deals with Public Safety

In many ways progressives are uncomfortable with the enforcement side of public safety. We know what we don't like—the death penalty, high incarceration rates, police abuse—but we are not entirely sure how to deal with the fact that there is actually a lot of violence, most of it in areas of the city where middle-class progressives do not live. So we talk as though an increase in human services would solve the entire problem. Then we support someone for mayor who has to run a real police department, and we cannot decide exactly what we want the person to do.

Dellums took this problem head on. "No one expects a progressive to make public safety first priority, but I intend to make it 'due North.'" Everything affects public safety and public safety affects everything. Dellums had a personal commitment to non-violence, but he had grown up in the 'hood, had been taught to defend himself by his wise Louisiana-born grandmother, and often talked with the families of young men who were killed on the streets.

Dellums had already participated in the enforcement side of government, serving in the Marines in his 20s and chairing the House Armed Services Committee toward the end of his tenure in Congress. His concentration on the issue paid off. During his time in office, the homicide rate dropped by an astonishing 40% (Gammon 2010c). Almost every other serious crime category saw a reduction. This chapter details Dellums's strategy for reducing the crime rate while dealing with the challenge of reforming a police department under court order to clean up its historic record of resident abuse.

The Issue of the Police

Every big city has police issues. Oakland's are well known. The Black Panther Party was organized at Merritt College in Oakland and became famous for asserting African Americans' right of self-defense. The Panthers carried out a famous protest that involved bringing unloaded guns into the state capitol to protest police brutality and selective enforcement of gun laws. The Panther protest reminded anyone prepared to think about it that, despite a mental image of "black violence" carried around by many Americans, cross-racial killings in the U.S. were primarily a white-on-black affair and included civilian lynchings in the South and police shootings in the North. FBI director J. Edgar Hoover did not see it that way and publicly interpreted the Panther stance as an attack on police and the social order. The FBI engaged in a well-documented campaign to discredit and destroy the Panthers (U.S. Senate 1976). In interesting contrast, when white suburbanites recently displayed their guns at local Starbucks, they were seen by many to be asserting their constitutional rights, the same Second Amendment rights the Panthers claimed with a different result.

Police activity in Oakland has stayed in the news. Very few Oakland police live in Oakland. In 2002 rogue police were accused of abusing residents of low-income communities. This became known as the Riders Case, and the department came under a court-monitored "negotiated settlement agreement" under which they were to make many reforms, including discipline of police who abused their position. Eight years later, Judge Thelton Henderson still did not consider the department sufficiently reformed. In 2009 the national public had watched an officer from another local police department (the BART police) shoot an unarmed twenty-year-old while he was was lying face down and handcuffed on an Oakland train platform.

People Want Crime Reduction

At the same time Oakland had a high homicide rate and residents wanted police action to deal with it. Dellums was an Oaklander, personally familiar with the history of Oakland's police department, but he was distressed by the homicide rate and believed that the black community, like other communities, wanted a fully staffed police department and a reduction in serious crime.

The essence of Dellums's strategy included the following points. The first three applied to his leadership style on most issues; the next six were specific to public safety.

Dellums's general approach to leadership:

1. Solve the problem; don't poke at it. "Bring me a solution that fits the size of the problem; not the size of the funding source" was a challenge he brought to all city department heads from the first few weeks of his administration. He did not want a few more police; he wanted a fully staffed police department.

2. Don't micromanage. Let the people you put in charge of things do their jobs. "Let the Chief be the Chief" became another Dellums mantra.

3. Give direction in private. He never, in my memory, critiqued anyone in public, even when such a critique would have been justified. The exception was the press, which he sometimes criticized because he thought they were unwilling to play a role in educating the community about the issues.

His specific approach to public safety:

4. The police should be required to do their jobs at the times and in the places they were needed. Management's right to make these decisions had been given up in previous police contracts. One highly placed, long-time city staffer who did not work for Mayor Dellums told me that "Over the years the City Council had given a lot to the Oakland Police Officers Association, including control over hours and staffing. Some of us worked for years on trying to change that. I was so impressed by the fact that Dellums was finally able to do it." One decision that helped make this happen was Dellums's retention of Chief Tucker, an older former sheriff and outsider in the police department, who seemed to share the "I'm too old to be intimidated" approach. (Retention of Tucker was a community task force recommendation). In March 2008, Dellums's push on this issue resulted in the city winning a legal ruling which restored management rights to the police department. (Gammon 2010c) In addition, the department implemented geographic accountability.

5. The police department needed to be at full staffing level (839 police) according to city policy. That staffing level was never achieved until Dellums made it a priority. He pushed past objections to the funding arrangement, and this also made it possible to actually hire one community policing officer for each beat for the first time since the community policing policy was created. When the national financial crisis threatened to decimate the new hires, Dellums's advocacy produced one of the largest

federal public safety grants in the country, $60 million over three years, which restored some of the cuts.

6. The department needed a strong and independent Chief. When Tucker retired, Dellums hired Anthony Batts, who had reduced crime as well as officer-involved shootings in Long Beach. Dellums credits Batts with continuing the decrease in serious crime even after the budget crises caused new reductions in police staffing (Gammon 2010a). At the same time it is important to note that serious crime, including homicides, was reduced every year during Dellums's tenure even before Batts was hired.

7. Policy and practice had to be put in place to assist the formerly incarcerated if these individuals were to become stable, contributing members of the community. "I came to the conclusion that if we relegated these people to the shadows of the economy, we were never going to bring down crime in this city," Dellums said (Gammon 2010a). Isaac Taggart was hired to coordinate those policy, employment, and counseling efforts as we will discuss later in this chapter.

8. In spite of the city's budget challenges the Parks and Recreation Department was one area that saw budget increases under Dellums. Dellums had worked as a recreation director himself during his college years, and he wanted many, many more things for young people to do.

9. Mayor Dellums took some steps to ensure the public safety of undocumented immigrants. He declared Oakland a "sanctuary city," which meant that police would not be actively assisting the Immigration and Naturalization Service with finding and deporting Oakland residents. He also directed police to allow individuals who were stopped without a license 30 minutes for a licensed relative to pick up the car before it was towed and stored or destroyed. This may seem like a small action to people with a driver's license, but it was major for a community which cannot afford the thousands of dollars in fines that result from having one's car towed.

10. Dellums also worked on economic development, the ultimate crime fighter. This topic is discussed in detail elsewhere, but it is worth noting here that Oakland is one of the few cities that saw job growth in spite of the downturn.

New Protests against Police

Many things have changed since the Panthers took on the issue of police abuse 45 years ago, but the vulnerability of young black men in relation to uniformed officers has not. In January 2009 Oscar Grant was killed by an officer of the Bay Area

Rapid Transit District Police Department, and the killing was captured on video and shown around the world. The protest was enormous and passionate. The officer who shot Grant received only a short prison term. The brevity of his sentence was a frightening symbol of their vulnerability for those young men forced to use the same trains and the same streets that Oscar Grant used. However, the protest could credit itself for creating the atmosphere in which Officer Mehserle was found guilty and served his prison term (even though it was a short one), given that white police rarely receive any punishment for killing black men.

Although the city of Oakland did not have jurisdiction and was not responsible, the protests ended up at City Hall. During some protests young whites from Ukiah, Oregon, and other distant non-urban spots showed up with masks and lethal Molotov cocktails, claiming the right to burn the cars and small businesses belonging to people who probably had a lot less money than they did, all in the name of "justice." I don't know what motivated them. I do know they have set a new challenge for those who want purposeful and organized protests.

Dellums took on the difficult challenge of responding as the executive who was in charge of protecting the city, while, at the same time, wanting young people to hear that he shared their exasperation and sadness. On the night of the first protest Dellums walked the streets with the protesters talking, empathizing, consoling, calming (Oakland Mayor Ron Dellums Tries to Calm the Crowd 2009).

During later protests he asked his office to help organize the community. The Parks department began holding the "healing circles" which had first been proposed by Kweli Tutashinda; Chinyere, his daughter; and the rest of the youth violence task force so that young and old had a place to talk. Isaac Taggart and several other courageous leaders set up a "peacekeepers" group. They wore orange vests and worked to make the protests orderly and peaceful. (The Panthers played a similar role during the urban rebellions of their era, urging people to protest without burning their own cities.)

The Public Safety Task Forces and How They Operated

Many of Mayor Dellums' actions were either proposed or endorsed by the public safety task forces. The community policing task force, for example, proposed the creation of a public safety director, a civilian who would work directly for the mayor, to coordinate all aspects of public safety, including, but not limited to, the police department. This would include civilian oversight of the police, work with City Council on the public safety strategy, neighborhood organizing for community policing, prevention and intervention activities, and so on. This very interesting task force included among its members a white lawyer, a young man returning to Oakland from incarceration, a music critic who had become political in the 1960s student movement, a public school teaching assistant who was also a neighborhood activist, and the white North Oakland small business owner sometimes thought of as the "father of community policing." The task force convener, Jeff Baker, understood how community policing was supposed to work and had carried out aspects of it as a city employee in South Berkeley a decade earlier. He believed that Oakland could be safer with fewer police after actually analyzing the assets and the problems of each community and helping the residents to use police services proactively (Heredia 2007b). Most of the recommendations of that task force were implemented, including the public safety director, and a declaration by the police chief, also a task force recommendation, that "every officer is a community policing officer."

After Mayor Dellums adopted the task force recommendation and hired a public safety director, he used the position to smash through legal and political barriers on the way to full staffing of the police department. Within a year and a half Oakland had a fully staffed police department of 839 officers for the first time in twenty years and one community policing officer for each beat. The mayor and police chief had declared "every officer a community policing officer," and Jeff Baker, the former task force convener, had been hired in the city administrator's office to manage the Measure Y Violence Prevention funds. The mayor had followed another of their recommendations by declaring public safety "due north," meaning that the city's public safety strategy would include a multi-pronged approach to jobs and services, in recognition of the fact that we "cannot arrest our way out of crime."

Although the task forces formally ended after the six initial sessions, the community policing task force continued meeting for five years! Their recommendations were adopted, but they were not convinced that the police were fully committed to real community policing, and they have continued to campaign for new forms of training and involvement of the residents.

Another successful public safety task force dealt with the "reintegration of incarcerated individuals," an issue that Dellums thought so important that he employed a re-entry specialist, an activist named Isaac Taggart. Isaac's history included owning an African American bookstore and organizing to shut down construction sites that did not hire black workers. Through his efforts every recommendation on re-entry was implemented. This included "banning the box" (on the city's job application that required disclosure of a felony arrest); producing a comprehensive resource guide; beginning the actual employment of the formerly incarcerated on city-funded projects; and obtaining several million dollars for a "day-reporting center" at a convenient location in Oakland (Hancox 2010).

A unique aspect of implementing the re-entry effort may have been the unspoken messages, however. The mayor assigned Isaac a spacious office in the middle of the mayoral suite of offices, and dozens of individuals recently released from prison were welcomed into the mayor's space each week, introduced to the mayor's staff and sometimes to the mayor himself. Treating the formerly incarcerated with respect was not a sidelight but a central aspect of creating a more just city.

The Post-Dellums Police Department

Oakland's police were back in the news in October 2011 when they beat and arrested the generally peaceful protestors of Occupy Oakland. Dellums's successor, Jean Quan, considers herself a progressive when it comes to policies on public safety, arguing for prevention more than suppression, but it remains to be seen whether she can control a police department which seems out of control to many, including the federal judge who is threatening to take it over.

7

Economic Engines for Old Industrial Cities:

The Port of Oakland

High unemployment in old industrial cities results from three realities:

1. Although many cities have a great deal of economic activity, the people who live in the city are often not hired on the jobs this activity creates. In areas ranging from teaching (the largest profession in the world) to construction jobs to work in high-end, high-tip restaurants, fewer African Americans are hired than their percentage in the population would suggest. Latinos are similarly affected by unemployment, particularly in the latest recession. Latinos are currently one-seventh of the labor force and one-fifth of the unemployed (Tan 2010).
2. Manufacturing industries have moved away from the cities, leaving areas like West Oakland with high unemployment.
3. What passes for a renaissance in some cities amounts to becoming a food and entertainment destination for non-residents or creating high-end residential development for those who wish to move back to the cities from the suburbs.

Oakland's situation is shaped by two others factors: one pushing toward "gentrification"; the other making possible the survival of a multi-racial working-class population. Oakland's proximity to San Francisco, its great weather, and its beautiful views create more pressure to become a bedroom community for San Francisco. However, on the other hand, the Oakland Port provides better built-in development possibilities than some cities possess for a natural and genuine expanding industry which could potentially (but not inevitably) employ its local residents.

A combination of forces, including the election of Dellums and the activity of the task forces, created momentum for a less-gentrifying set of solutions. The economic development task forces included several hundred individuals and made many important recommendations. This chapter and the next will highlight four of their approaches and the results. (See www.oacp.net for a complete summary of their recommendations.)

My coverage is in no way intended to dismiss the significance of other individual and community efforts on these issues, but the task force impetus did push some ideas over the top which had been languishing for years.

Margaret Gordon: Symbol of a New Approach to the Port

The Port of Oakland is a huge economic enterprise which has brought jobs and commodities to Northern California and beyond for a hundred years. It has also made a lot of people sick, a large portion of them the African American residents of Oakland's flatlands.

Campaigning against that sickness has been the work of West Oakland resident, Margaret Gordon, who stands as a model of both grassroots activism and participatory research. Margaret has lived in West Oakland most of her life. She has asthma as do three of her ten grandchildren. She joined a project to research health indicators for her West Oakland community during the 1990s and organized the West Oakland Environmental Indicators Project, which helped residents to research air quality. In 1998 the resident-researchers discovered that West Oakland had the highest level of toxic air releases in the city and that children in West Oakland were seven times more likely to have asthma than other children in California. Their first campaign targeted the worst single emitter, the Red Yeast factory. In 2003 that company shut down, and the community began working on Port emissions issues, which included the emissions of ships and of trucks traveling to and from the Port and idling in the neighborhood.

In order to get a close look at the number of truck trips and their locations, residents stood on corners and counted trucks that went by. Brian Beveridge, the co-director of the Environmental Indicators Project, says of Gordon that she is tireless and she believes in self-education. She has become a scientific expert in spite of the fact that she was not formally educated in that field. She teaches others by saying, "You need to see it, lay your hands on it, see it in context. And you can't expect somebody to do it all for you. You have to commit some time to your own self-education" (Oakland, Be a Good Citizen in the Fight for Health 2010).

In 2006 Margaret served as one of the conveners of mayor-elect Dellums's Port task force along with former Port executive director, Chuck Foster, and West Oakland businessman-turned-activist, Steve Lowe. The recommendations of that task force included prioritizing West Oakland community participation, jobs, and air quality. And they recommended that a resident of the "front-line" communities be appointed to the board of Port commissioners for the first time in history.

Symbolism and Substance: Dellums's First Appointment to the Port Commission

The Port of Oakland includes 665 acres of marine terminals, the 2,500-acre Oakland International Airport, 569 acres of commercial, industrial and recreational land under lease or available for lease or sale, and 9,700 acres that are presently under water (Port of Oakland website). Its net assets are valued at $890 million dollars (Port of Oakland website).

Although Oakland has always had a diverse population, prior to 1981 every member of the Oakland Port commission was white and male. In 1927 this group included the former governor of California, the owner of a major department store, a prominent attorney, a well-known pharmacist and the proprietor of a downtown tobacco shop (Port of Oakland website 2011).

Other cities still have port commissions that are completely white and male. The Baltimore Port is governed by a group of five individuals—four men, several CEOs, and no African Americans. The Port of San Diego's board has a similar composition and so does the Port of New York.

In the twenty-five years following Oakland's intense push for civil rights, 1981 to 2007, women, union leaders, Asians, and African Americans have been appointed. However, although the Port sits in West Oakland and profoundly affects it, no West Oakland resident had ever been appointed to its governing board.

On February 16, 2006, mayoral candidate Dellums and Margaret Gordon spoke at a conference sponsored by the Intermodal Maritime Association. Many of the attendees were truckers who would be greatly affected by new air quality regulations. Dellums was impressed by Margaret's detailed knowledge of Port issues and her ability to make common cause with a group so different from herself. He confided shortly thereafter that he intended her to be his first appointment to the

Port commission and that he was excited for the opportunity to carry out this community task force recommendation by appointing the first resident of West Oakland to this very powerful board.

He made the appointment in late summer of 2007, pending approval by the Oakland City Council. In one of those complex reactions I have noted about "progressives" in the U.S., some who considered Margaret to be a fine organizer were not supportive of her rise to a position of authority over the multi-million dollar enterprise of the Port of Oakland, even though the operations of the Port were killing her family and her neighbors. One leader reportedly commented that Ms. Gordon would not be "comfortable" with all those powerful people on the board.

Perhaps the best response was by African American business leader, Joe Debro, in a 2007 article for the *San Francisco Bay View*. I quote him at length because his views represent much of importance about Oakland struggles over both ideas and economics:

> Unfortunately, the quality of a mind is too often measured by the amount of formal education surrounding it. One of the biggest mistakes of my life was to evaluate the quality of my father's mind based on his lack of formal education. I came to the conclusion that I was smarter because I had degrees and he did not. It took me 50 years to understand the folly of my conclusion. The current stewards of the public trust at the Port of Oakland all have degrees. These well-educated commissioners agreed to virtually give away Port land and other Port real estate in the past several years. In violation of both city and state laws, they awarded the largest no-bid construction contract in the history of the City of Oakland to Turner Construction Co. for $300 million. Neither they nor the professionals whom they supervise have a clue regarding the cost of the improvements which they have authorized at the Airport. Their handling of the concessions at the Port has shown a careless disregard for the needs of the citizens of Oakland. They appear to sell any asset of the Port for a price below market value and buy any service for prices above retail value. Can a less educated Port commissioner improve on that record? Margaret Gordon, Mayor Ron Dellums' nominee for the Board of Port Commissioners, is being opposed partly because of her relative lack of formal education. The City Council has approved nominees who allegedly did not meet the charter requirement of residency. It approved all of former Mayor Jerry Brown's nominees without question. Why would the Council oppose Dellums' first significant appointment? (Debro 2007)

There was intense organizing by environmentalists; West Oakland residents; and others to ensure Gordon's approval, and ultimately the City Council did vote to approve her appointment.

Since Margaret's appointment, the Port of Oakland has passed the Maritime Air Quality Plan. Neither Margaret nor many community activists considered the plan sufficiently stringent, but trucks are being retrofitted; diesel emissions have been reduced somewhat; and American President Lines have begun "cold-ironing" ships while they are in Port, which is projected to reduce particulates by 1500 tons per year.

Obviously, Margaret was not the only force behind the change. Other Dellums Port commission appointees, cooperation from the federal Environmental Protection Agency, and the Bay Area Air Quality Management District as well as present and potential lawsuits and ongoing community pressure have all played a part. Still, Ms. Gordon's role has been pivotal and Dellums' willingness to break through the class-based assumptions about who belonged on the Port Commission have created a new set of assumptions about how the economic world should work.

Dellums made other appointments that represent different backgrounds than those found on other port commissions around the country: Michael Lighty, the passionate head of the California Nurses Association; long-time community leader, James Head, who is also the executive director of the San Francisco Foundation; Gilda Gonzalez, a leader of the Latino-serving organization, the Unity Council; and Pam Calloway, who has a background in workforce development.

Margaret reports that there have been important changes, in addition to the air quality plan as a result of the new appointments: greater scrutiny of Port finances, a particular interest of Mr. Lighty; personnel audits, motivated by Ms. Calloway; and so on (personal interview, June 2, 2011).

Growing the Port

Making the Port environmentally safe is one part of serving Oakland residents. The other aspect is making it an engine for job development. If Margaret Gordon's appointment to the Port commission symbolized one side of that equation, the struggle over the use of the Army base is the other side.

Oakland has been trying to figure out how to use its old Army base since it was decommissioned in 1999. The base opened in December 1941, one day after the attack on Pearl Harbor, and sent 25 million tons of supplies and tens of thousands of soldiers to war during its 58 years of existence.

Oakland has considered a number of uses for it since 1999, including potential use as an entertainment facility to be built by the Wayans Brothers. By the time Dellums took office, the Wayans deal was almost dead.

At that point Dellums asked for proposals for Army base use and appointed a group to review them. The group recommended a proposal submitted by AMB Property Corporation and California Capital Group for a trade and logistics center adjacent to the Port. It would potentially create 3,000 immediate jobs through infrastructure improvement and 12,000 long-term jobs related to goods movement, technology research and development (State of the City 2007–2011, p. 15).

By the time the proposals were submitted and reviewed, Dellums had made a strategic decision about Port development which coincided with the recommendations of the group making the review. He had decided that Port-related logistics was a better use of the former Army Base than retail or other possible uses. In early 2009 Ports America had signed a 50-year agreement for Outer Harbor, Berths 20–24, which contributed to his decision on this matter. The length of the agreement was unprecedented and was interpreted by Port Executive Director Omar Benjamin as an indication of the Oakland Port's long-term potential growth (Port Press Release 2009). In conversation with Ports America officials, Dellums concluded that Oakland's geographic position gave it enormous long-term potential as a leading international port and that the absolute best use of the Army base would be to support that growth.

Although I was not sure if I agreed with him at the time, I have since become convinced that he was right. The working-class jobs available through this development are the best hope for Oakland to employ its current residents and maintain its quality as the "gritty, working class cousin" embodied in Shawn Ginwright's quote.

But it is not a foregone conclusion that Oaklanders, especially the unemployed residents of East and West Oakland, will get these jobs. And Margaret Gordon is once again the person raising a cautionary voice. Interviewed by a reporter in 2010 about her impressions of the Army base project, Gordon said, "The numbers of African American people who get the jobs or contracts on this project—from the time of digging in the dirt to see how tainted it is, to putting in the infrastructure to putting in the vertical and horizontal development to getting the construction jobs—I can't predict. Because I've been on so many major projects in West Oakland for the past 18 years, and it never pans out. For the Cypress Freeway, which was a billion-dollar project, we've only proved that 65 people in 94607, 94608 (West Oakland) zip codes got jobs" (Mullane 2010).

Ms. Gordon, in alliance with representatives of several West Oakland organizations, the Oakland Black Caucus, Black Women Organized for Political Action, and eight or nine other groups, formed a coalition to make sure that the employment result would be better this time around. The Coalition, OaklandWORKS, has already had a big impact on city policy as reflected in the staff report on Army base jobs in the appendices.

Margaret Gordon has also become a national leader, honored by Oprah's *O* magazine and television program, awarded the prestigious Promise Prize, and invited by activists in other cities to "help us get someone like you on our Port Commission."

8

Jobs: Three Local Policies That Make a Difference for the 99%

"Gritty Cities" Need Industrial Land Use Policies

Land use policy is not on the nightly news, but it is key to maintaining a working-class city. The other options, given a U.S. capitalist framework, are a downtrodden, out-of-work city or a gentrified Disneyland, which houses only the affluent and those who service them.

There is a long-term struggle, highlighted by the Occupy Wall Street Movement, for the creation of an economy which sustains humanity and the planet, because it is driven by actual human need, rather than ever-more profitable and unnecessary disposable consumption. If this broad international movement is successful there may finally be a serious discussion of whether or not profit should determine the distribution of human resources.

In the meantime, within the context of the current system, we will have to aim for industries that produce products that are at least minimally useful and policies to employ and house those who have not been able to gain employment because of systematic barriers.

This story about business owner Rich Bourdon makes clear why land use policy matters to job-creating business. Bourdon owned a business in San Francisco. He moved it to Oakland because he says the "market rate" (more affluent) housing residents who moved in near his business in San Francisco complained about the "noise and smells." Bourdon now employs 100 union workers in Oakland in his custom woodworking business. He worries that what happened in San

Francisco could happen again in Oakland, if the City Council allowed new residential development in the area around his business (Burt & Rayburn 2008).

The average Oakland resident either needs a job or has a family member who needs one and cannot afford the new market-rate housing which is built if zoning for business is not prioritized. All but the most affluent Oaklanders are better off with an "industrial zoning" policy that protects business from the situation Bourdon describes.

Two of the Dellums task forces (housing and land use) urged a strong industrial land use policy. They recognized that on this issue they had potential allies in labor and the Metropolitan Chamber of Commerce. They asked Mayor Dellums to issue a statement supporting this policy recommendation and asked the Central Labor Council and the Chamber of Commerce to join them in a press release. Then they pushed the City Council for approval. In March 2008, they issued the following statement:

> Only five percent (5%) of the remaining land over which the City Council has authority is industrial-use land. Such lands comprise the physical space where businesses are or will be based, and from which economic development and job growth must come. A policy that provides strong protections for industrial land, discouraging spot rezoning for residential construction, will protect businesses already in our city and lay the basis for future economic growth in Oakland. (Mayor Dellums Presents Industrial Land Use 2008)

It worked. Their action combined with the earlier organizing of council member Nancy Nadel and advocacy group, Just Cause, got an industrial land use policy passed on March 5, 2008 (Taylor 2008). It involved a compromise which made the policy less than perfect. Nadel wanted the industrial space in her district protected; Council member De la Fuente wanted residential development, rather than industrial use, in the Tidewater area of his district. The two council members made a compromise which protected most industrial land in the city but allowed De la Fuente a carve-out for the Tidewater area in order for Nadel to get enough votes for passage (Burt & Rayburn 2008). *Tribune* reporter Cecil Burt summarized the compromise like this, "The Oakland City Council voted to protect hundreds of acres of industrially zoned land early Wednesday, but not before siding with developers who want to build housing in a heavily industrialized area of the Central Waterfront" (Burt & Rayburn 2008).

This action indicates the difference that the participatory planning and action process of the task forces made at critical junctures. The language of the community task forces on land use and housing was developed with great care by individuals like Mel Blair, Bob Schwartz, Sandi Galvez, Margot Prada, Aisha Brown, Norm Hooks, Ray Carlisle, Robyn Hodges, and others. And task force members—businessperson Steve Lowe, Green Studies professor, Robin Freeman, and others—pushed the press release and joint action that finally got council action on this long-standing issue.

Activist organizations like Urban Habitat, also praised Mayor Dellums and the task forces for slowing the conversion of industrial land which had been rampant between 1998 and 2005 because of the willingness of the planning commission to allow exceptions to the city's existing land use and transportation plan

In addition to its policy significance, the vote demonstrates the importance of the 2006 and 2010 mayoral elections. A De la Fuente mayorship in 2006 or the election of his ally, Don Perata, in 2010 would have favored the continuation of high-end residential development and the resulting gentrification. Residential developers earn greater profits than job-producing businesses and are therefore able to pay more for land and handsomely reward their political allies. This puts enormous pressure on the politicians of many cities to agree to high-end residential development.

Local Hire Policy—Historic Decision

A group of academics called "critical race theorists" argue that policies are not adopted in the U.S. to help non-whites unless there is "interest convergence," which means that the policy must also help whites. I would like them to be wrong, but I fear they are mostly right. There are, of course, many examples of individual whites who act as allies to people of color, but it is hard to find examples of policies that rectify long-standing economic injustice accepted by whites. Even the election of Barack Obama, which I do believe was an anti-racist milestone in U.S. history, was still supported by only 43% of whites. Reparations and what is termed "affirmative action" are two examples of policies which have either been rejected or drastically challenged because, in general, whites can find no benefit to themselves. Yet, there is a long history of policies which provided "affirmative action" to whites in the accumulation of assets (slavery, sharecropping, and the Homestead Act to name just three).

Non-white, low-wealth city families face numerous barriers to employment—decreased number of local jobs, direct discrimination, lack of transportation to other cities where jobs may exist, lack of access to white-dominated networks of information about jobs, lack of educational credentials, forms of standardized testing which invariably favor whites, language requirements, and so on.

For cities, the policy of requiring a certain percentage of local residents to be hired on publicly funded projects seems to have enough "interest convergence" that it will be acceptable to white residents as a policy. Whites who live in the city in question are likely to support it, because they will obtain some of the jobs, and there is an instant logic to the idea that projects funded by the taxes of city residents should hire city residents, no matter the inclination of the individual contractor.

One of the Dellums task forces proposed that the city's policy become 50% local hire with none of the "escape clauses" contractors sometimes promote. In December 2010, Mayor Dellums reaffirmed the policy of 50% local hire and directed its implementation.

Immediately, the percentage of local residents hired went up. However, the percentage of African Americans was still dismal, and a community-based organizing campaign has begun to rectify that aspect of the problem; the organizers include many of the original task force members. Because of discrimination, few African Americans are hired on construction jobs either within or outside the city, and the lack of employment in lucrative industries like construction is seen to be a major contributor to low income among African Americans. So this approach is an important one to utilize.

Mayor Dellums at press conference opening the new Business Assistance Center, a task force recommendation.

Long-Awaited Small Business Assistance

The final policy was a focus on the small businesses which create most of the jobs in the country and two-thirds of the jobs in Oakland. A Business Assistance Center was another desire of many Oakland residents and City Council members. The Dellums task force on small business proposed the center and then moved it forward with painstaking advocacy. Aziz Khatri, Larry Chang, Lynette Neidhardt, Boku Kodama, and a dozen other persistent souls helped the council and the staff to make it happen. It now stands proudly on Frank Ogawa Plaza and has already helped more than a thousand businesses. Mike McPherson became its first director; his passing in 2011 was mourned by hundreds and hundreds of the people he had served. This very multi-racial task force also proposed the creation of 100 new black businesses, a proposal which is now being revived by the OaklandWORKS Coalition.

The emphasis on small business has been validated again by a new study which shows that startups and small businesses create 3 million jobs each year while the large industries lose a million jobs a year.

9

Economic Development:
Progressives and the Chamber of Commerce

Progressives have almost as much trouble figuring out how to work with Chambers of Commerce as we do with police departments. There are good reasons for the frequent antagonism. The National Chamber's position on taxes, for example, states that the country should "reduce the budget deficit through higher economic growth, spending restraint, and entitlement reform—not higher taxes," rejecting our of hand the need to tax in a different way the blooming garden of new billionaires. Locally, the Oakland Chamber has often supported the candidates who were least progressive on social issues and appealed to the narrowest interests of business.

But soon after Dellums was elected it was clear that his national stature and reach could assist Oakland business. The Metropolitan Chamber began working on an "Oakland Partnership," which included the mayor's office, the Chamber, labor representatives, and others. The mayor insisted that it also include the "ethnic" Chambers of Commerce (African American, Vietnamese, Hispanic) and the task forces.

The Metropolitan Chamber had employed an unusually talented economic development director, Karen Engel, who had a social justice conscience and the ability to work flexibly with many people.

Some progressives complained to Dellums that the proposed Oakland Partnership would give the Chamber too much power. I appreciated their concerns, but I could see that a mayor with an egalitarian reputation, trying to create socially useful jobs in a big city, would have to do something with business, and it would likely be most successful in an organized, purposeful, and public setting. The current questions had to focus on the content of the proposals: What industries? Producing what products and services? Benefiting whom? Creating how many jobs? Hiring who and at what kind of wages? And who would participate in the process?

The Metropolitan Chamber had commissioned a study called the McKinsey Report which developed some conclusions that were compatible with the task force process including the notion that healthcare, the arts, international trade and logistics, and green industry were critical to Oakland's future. The McKinsey Report added biotechnology, which was not among those industries analyzed by the task forces.

An Oakland Partnership was formed; the Chamber of Commerce report written a year later described its development this way: "On the basis of the work by McKinsey as well as the work of hundreds of community volunteers on the community task forces convened by the mayor, the Chamber and the mayor and a number of other stakeholders came together to form the Oakland Partnership." The Chamber acknowledged that the Oakland Partnership had created "significant" results (Engel 2008). (There are lots of "partnerships" described in this book; I hope the reader will be able to keep them straight!)

Unlike the task force process, which aimed for collective consensus policy making on the part of ordinary residents, the industry-based cluster process spearheaded by Karen Engel was interested in engaging the leaders of various companies and institutions and encouraging them to throw the weight of their institutions in a particular direction. In the case of healthcare, the chairs were Frank Tiedeman, the CEO of Children's Hospital and Bette Coles, the senior vice president of Kaiser Permanente. The chairs of the international trade and logistics cluster were the CEO of the Port of Oakland and the director of PACAM, a rapidly growing logistics and warehousing company. The Oakland Partnership drew in other industry leaders and worked with them to overcome barriers in the growth of that industry. It included input from the community task force reports and many task force members joined the industry clusters. The whole project was assisted in this strategy by a group with some interesting international development ideas, called the Economic Competitiveness Group.

The cluster strategy had many successes; one example was enormously important to Port development. The trade and logistics cluster recognized that the Port of Oakland could grow significantly if the goods reaching the Port could get to the rest of the U.S. That meant "infrastructure development," so that goods could pass through those big mountains on the eastern side of California: "Make the Maritime Port a First Port of Call by addressing infrastructure issues: (1) funding and building rail access improvements at Donner Pass (allowing double-stacked rail cars); the Tehachapi Pass (double track); and the Martinez subdivision. . . ." The cluster worked hard on this, and, at the very end of 2009, the railroad had actually raised the ceilings of its tunnels at Donner Pass to allow double-stacked rail cars (Voyles 2010). This route is 78 miles shorter than the previous Feather River Route and allows Union Pacific to offer 9000-foot trains, a 58% increase over the length of trains through the Feather River Route (Boyd 2009, Nov. 24). (A visual of the double stacked trains is available on YouTube http://www.youtube.com/watch?v=O Tt9EFBwqRE)

In their 2009 two-year progress report the clusters listed many other accomplishments. The International Trade and Logistics Cluster reported $3 billion in Port-related investments; completion of the maritime air quality improvement plan; a $10 million grant to retrofit older trucks; a successful biofuel pilot project; and new workforce development projects with Department of Labor funding.

The health care cluster recorded success in the training of bilingual healthcare personnel, the completion of a Kaiser Hospital medical office building; the securing of $98 million for Children's Hospital; and expanded nursing programs at area hospitals.

In this second year report, the Oakland Partnership reported the following on their key goals: $5 billion in investment to key sectors; expanded workforce development through Peralta Colleges and their community-based partners, and "on track for the creation of 10,000 new jobs, despite the recession."

The success of the Oakland Partnership must be attributed, at least partly, to the fact that almost every major player in each of the economic development areas was at the table with the mayor and the consultants airing the difficulties they were facing in achieving each major goal. There could be immediate action—a phone call from the mayor, a letter from the director of the Port, an action by one of the shipping companies—to implement the goals.

Assessing the Implications from a Progressive Point of View

Mayor Dellums made clear from his early campaign speeches that he was not "antidevelopment." His criteria for development were that it should benefit the existing residents and "everyone should have a seat at the table" in decision making. This had implications both large and small. The "seat at the table" took many forms:

The task force members themselves were important members of the cluster working groups, even though they were not, for the most part, CEOs themselves. The task force recommendations were part of the decision-making materials.

1. The Oakland Partnership's yearly conferences provided hundreds of complimentary tickets to ordinary residents; many of whom had been active in the task force process. Attending a conference may seem unimportant, but most of these residents had never been invited to a luncheon at the Marriott Hotel, had never met city staff or business leaders, had never heard the actual arguments in favor of various economic policies.

2. Each presentation panel was unusually diverse and included the most egalitarian perspectives. At each economic summit meeting, task force representatives shared the stage with CEOs and bankers.

3. The economic development plan for the city was being made in a public venue with publicly available reports on a public stage with hundreds of ordinary residents in attendance.

10

Education and the City

Thank you to the Spanish Speaking Citizens Foundation for permission to use their beautiful mural.

The education history of northern U.S. cities is filled with myths. Many believe that the 20th century was a period of democratic, well-functioning racially integrated school systems, educating most children efficiently and effectively. Oakland's history is a good example of some contrary truths.

Oakland School History

During the period when the corporate influence of Southern Pacific and the *Oakland Tribune* was increasing citywide, a more corporate and stratified school district was also being created. Superintendent Fred Hunter brought race-based tracking to the Oakland schools during the 1920s through his collaboration with Lewis Terman, a Stanford professor and eugenics advocate (Terman 1916). Oakland became one of the first districts in the country to use Terman's newly created group I.Q. test to track its classes. Superintendent Hunter actually employed Terman's graduate assistant, Virgil Dickson, as the research director for the Oakland School District.

Terman's racial views are made clear in a quote from his *The Measurement of Intelligence* (1916):

> Among laboring men and servant girls there are thousands like them (feebleminded individuals). They are the world's "hewers of wood and drawers of water." And yet, as far as intelligence is concerned, the tests have told the truth . . . No amount of school instruction will ever make them intelligent voters or capable voters in the true sense of the word. . . . The fact that one meets this type with such frequency among Indians, Mexicans, and Negroes suggests quite forcibly that the whole question of racial differences in mental traits will have to be taken up anew and by experimental methods. (Terman 1916, pp. 91–92)

By 1925, 215 other city school districts were also using Terman's I.Q. test.

Superintendent Hunter's policy-making reflected other conservative practices. Oakland had been the location one of the first suffragette marches in the country, but Superintendent Hunter required teachers to attend a mandatory speech by a prominent anti-suffrage advocate. Muckraker Upton Sinclair, author of *The Jungle*, the book which stimulated meat-packing regulation, also authored *The Goslings*, a book on education that featured Oakland. Sinclair called Hunter "a pawn" of construction contractors. When Oakland voted $5 million for new schools, Hunter constructed an oversight committee which included only businessmen. When some of the school board members objected, Hunter used the *Oakland Tribune* to campaign for their replacement by a more pliable board (Sinclair 1924).

Race, Economy, and Education

Like other cities', Oakland's population was growing rapidly and becoming more diverse. Most of the population was working class; tens of thousands were employed by Durant Motor Company, Union Iron Works, Southern Pacific, and similar companies. African Americans and Asians made up ten percent of the population. A strict segregation policy was enforced. A leaflet distributed in the Rockridge Area in 1911 said, "It is probably unnecessary even to mention that no one of African or Mongolian descent will even be allowed to own a lot in Rockridge or rent a house that may be built there" (Bagwell 1996, p. 206).

The Oakland schools, which had 12,000 students in 1900, had over 48,000 by 1918, the same period during which the testing and tracking practices were started. Jobs in growing industries were drawing rural whites and Southern African Americans (Wilkerson 2011). Education policy makers considered this growth to be reason for the separation and stratification of children. The idea that children of all races would be taught in the same classes was actually no more acceptable to policy makers in the North than the South. Academics like Elwood Cubberly, a colleague of Terman's at Stanford, created a system which depended not on legal segregation but on "scientific assessment." Cubberly's writings influenced generations of superintendents and principals, and there are still buildings and schools named for him in Palo Alto, California, the location of Stanford University. He said "Our city schools will soon be forced to give up the exceedingly democratic idea that all are equal and our society devoid of classes . . . and to begin a specialization of educational effort along many lines in an attempt to adapt the school to the needs of these many classes" (Cubberly 1916, p. 338).

Terman explained that "mental tests given to nearly 30,000 children in Oakland prove conclusively that the proportion of failures due chiefly to mental inferiority is nearer 90 percent than 50 percent" (Tyack 1974, p. 209). They constructed five tracks from "accelerated" to "atypical" and also made a push for vocational education beginning in 1925.

There was opposition. Oakland's first black teacher and a masters student at U.C. Berkeley, Ida Jackson, said, "In many schools the Principal and many of the teachers do not believe in the validity of the intelligence tests" (Jackson 1923).

Oakland was not the only city to use IQ testing and ability grouping. By 1925, 215 cities used intelligence tests. Of 40 cities with a population of at least 100,000, 37 used "ability" grouping in 1926. Secondary schools used the tests to organize ability grouping and to guide the choice of careers (Tyack 1974, p. 208). Since ability was always defined by the newly created standardized tests and test score always correlated with family wealth, this meant that students were segregated by their parents' social class.

The tracked approach to education stayed in place until the Civil Rights Movement, when the city began electing school board directors that reflected its ethnic composition. By the time 60% of Oakland students were African American, the majority of the school board was also black and began passing resolutions against tracking and racially biased textbooks and in favor of respect for African-influenced English. In 1997 Oakland made national headlines with the "Ebonics Resolution" affirming African American language and espousing the idea that children should be explicitly taught the value of their home language and the ability to switch to "Standard American" English.

State officials, including then State Superintendent Bill Honig began working with a few locals to seize control of the Oakland district and return things to what they considered financially and educationally proper. There were three separate attempts to take over the district. Oakland was one of many African American majority school districts ultimately taken over; however it was the only one to successfully resist the takeover for fifteen years (Epstein 2012).

The champions of the first two takeovers claimed financial and educational problems, but there was considerable local opposition and the school board retained local control. When Jerry Brown became mayor, he and State Senator Don Perata insisted on choosing a new superintendent (Dennis Chaconas) to replace popular, long-time educator Carole Quan. The district shortly thereafter showed a deficit, and state takeover action was initiated by Don Perata. There was again great opposition to this third takeover attempt, but the deficit, though disputed, was sufficiently large to convince the state legislature to approve Perata's bill to impose a large loan and state takeover. The district was run for six years by an administrator appointed by the state superintendent and a state government which was, like most state governments, not ethnically representative of its major cities.

State control of the school district did not end until Dellums became mayor, and his former aide, Sandre Swanson, was elected to the State Assembly. One of Dellums's first actions as mayor-elect was a car trip to Sacramento for a chat with the state superintendent during which he informed Jack O'Connell that he wanted the city to run its own schools and he did not want the state to sell the district's central office property, a step that was rumored to be imminent, as real estate owned by the public was too precious to be sold for short-term financial relief. Sandre Swanson's first action as a State Assembly member, was introduction of a bill to return local control to the district.

O'Connell had aleady talked about eventual return of control; these events seemed to prompt a shorter timeline. The school board chose Tony Smith, who had worked previously in both Oakland and San Francisco, as its new superintendent. When the takeover ended in 2008 the district had a debt larger than the deficit which caused the takeover in the first place; a higher rate of teacher turnover; a proliferation of charter schools which were partly responsible for a 30% decrease in the district's student population; an improved set of central office systems, and a continuation of some school reforms started before the takeover (a concession negotiated by reform activists, including the Oakland Coalition of Community Organizations). In addition, a portion of the citizenry was so outraged that they were prepared to campaign against anything with Don Perata's name attached.

The Mayor and the Schools

Ironically, at his first meeting with U.S. Secretary of Education Arne Duncan, Dellums along with 20 or 30 other mayors heard Duncan explain why the mayors themselves should take over their school districts. Given Oakland's experience with state take-over and his own inclinations toward democratic and broadly distributed governance, Mayor Dellums did not support this policy and was more interested in figuring out how the city could wrap its arms around the schools, rather than taking them over.

Several Oakland organizations had been working on a proposal to Atlantic Philanthropies for school-based health centers. Oakland already had several high school health centers; the new proposal would create centers at a majority of the middle schools. Atlantic Philanthropies met with Mayor Dellums and informed him that his election as mayor increased their interest in Oakland as a site for these projects because they knew his long history of effective public health advocacy. County, Kaiser-Permanente and school construction funding were brought together with the Atlantic Philanthropies grant to create one of the most extensive networks of urban school-based health care in the country. The whole project is administered by Safe Passages, a large non-profit which has run many after school and other programs in tandem with the school district.

Dellums was also interested in reducing the drop-out rate and recruiting teachers who would be effective for Oakland students. For the first time in Oakland history, the mayor hosted a teacher recruitment fair in City Hall, explaining to the hundreds of attendees that teaching was an important and attractive career for Oakland residents and that students needed to have more teachers who looked like themselves. The task forces had proposed mechanisms to create a diverse teaching force (see Chapter 11); administrator Laura Moran at the school district was supportive; and the mayor wanted it to happen. So Teach Tomorrow in Oakland was born, one of the few programs that is explicitly devoted to diversity in the teaching force. The approach is strategically important for the overall improvement of U.S. education. The situation of Latinos in California provides just one stark example. Latinos are 51% of the students and only 16% of the teachers. A new teacher (Marisol Nuno) told me that she had not had a single Latino teacher before she was sixteen; that Israel Macias who taught her high school social studies class was pivotal in her life; and that she would not have become a teacher herself without this experience.

But the impact on individual students is just one reason teacher diversity is important. Teaching is one of the largest professions in the world. We have already discussed the barriers which prevent the black, Asian, and Latino populations from entering the teaching profession. These barriers contribute to the on-going unemployment and wealth gap issues we have already discussed. It is expensive to become a public school teacher, particularly when you consider that the starting pay in many states is less than $40,000 a year. The most restrictive requirement for new teachers is the necessity of teaching for free for a year as a student teacher. The racial wealth gap makes this impossible for many families. In addition, California, for example, requires four separate multi-part exams costing several hundred dollars. And these tests, like all norm-referenced standardized tests, have a disparate impact on different ethnicities (Epstein 2012).

Furthermore, the sort of welcoming, culturally competent, community-connected schools which can keep youngsters attending and growing need a multi-racial teaching force. Over 70% of the teachers in the U.S. are monolingual whites. We, the 70%, need day-to-day coaching from a set of colleagues who have other backgrounds.

A related program, Pathways to Teaching, also initiated by the mayor's office, uses "gang-prevention" funding in a unique model which provides youth engagement specialists; an introduction to college and stipend-supported employment, so that youngsters who might otherwise be victims of violence or gang recruitment can begin a pathway toward teaching or employment in community service. The program is informally linked to Teach Tomorrow in Oakland.

The mayor's office also sponsored events to link city, school district, Housing Authority and county staff. Parks Department staff, for example, often see young people who have dropped out of school; knowing teachers and being familiar with programs helps them to intervene. The Housing Authority is home to 30%

of Oakland public school students. Yet resources have not always been well coordinated.

The mayor's office sponsored many events directly to show that the city did not need to run the schools in order to help them. There were parent seminars to look at early chronic absenteeism; a graduation ceremony for a black independent school, Ile Omode; graduation ceremonies for a Latino Youth Engagement program called Libre; and a gathering of adult school teachers and Chinatown students who were protesting the elimination of their programs. The mayor's office also started a drop-out reduction program with a grant from America's Promise Alliance.

What the Occupy Movement Could Mean for the Schools

Thus far the Occupy protests have explicitly opposed school closings and the general privatization of education. But a far broader critique is made possible by this new conversation. Many concepts in U.S. education are drawn directly from corporate thinking and permeate assumptions about the country's goals for its children: "success" as the goal of school, "Racing to the Top," accountability, strategic planning, parents as customers, human capital, and a hundred other terms reflect the idea of the school as a business and the student as a product. The best educational environments (including the private schools where the wealthy send their own children) do not have this approach. Happiness, fulfillment, stimulation, cooperation and "developmentally appropriate" are contrasting concepts which may receive more attention now that a new movement is questioning the application of the business paradigm to all phenomena.

In the next chapter educator and activist Kimberly Mayfield Lynch describes the impact which connecting educators to City Hall had on her life and work.

11

Reflections of an Activist: Kimberly Mayfield Lynch[1]

Luvella Strawder Gary was born on March 2, 1906, in Rayville, Louisiana—a small feisty woman, and my maternal grandmother. I called her "Grandma Doll." I grew up hearing my parents talk about how she organized the women in her circle at church to vote from the 1960s through the 1980s. She told them about the issues, registered them to vote, and coordinated transportation to get them to the polls on Election Day. With an eleventh grade education, my Grandma Doll understood the value of the right to vote, community organizing and democracy. I believe I inherited these sensibilities from her. These sensibilities allowed me to recognize the importance of a Dellums' mayoral administration in Oakland. (Mayfield 2007)

When I was a student at the University of California at Santa Barbara from 1984–1988, I was steeped in the struggle for divestment from South Africa. One of the most vocal advocates for divestment was my congressman, Ronald V. Dellums. He was a fierce opponent of apartheid and was deeply committed to the release of Nelson Mandela as well as a pacifist and a supporter of universal health care. Because he was trained as a social worker, he understood basic human needs and worked to address them in Congress. Known for building multiracial coalitions, he was a true personification of the liberal politics of the San Francisco Bay Area. I was proud to live in the 9th Congressional District and to have him representing my interests in Washington. As a Black Studies and political science major,

I was well versed in historical political movements and the struggle for civil rights and human rights. I was inspired by the work of the Black Power Movement, especially the work of the Black Panther Party. I longed for an activist moment shaped by the passion and politics of the 1960s.

In the fall of 2005, I learned that Geoffrey Pete, Oakland businessman, had suggested that Dellums should run for mayor of the City of Oakland at a public event. The idea caught on like wildfire. With the mayoral election a year away, a group of progressive Oakland citizens devised a strategy to draft Dellums for mayor. The organizers of the Draft Dellums for Mayor campaign felt that his leadership and vision would bring back a sense of hope and possibility to the city. For the first time in years, citizens were active, enthusiastic, and passionate about a potential candidate. Approximately 9,000 people signed a petition urging the former congressman to run for mayor. I was one of the first people to solicit signatures. I even had my 71-year-old mother take a petition to her senior exercise class at the Golden Age Activity Center at the Eastmont Mall. She got all of the members in her class to sign. My father, a man of few words, began soliciting votes for Dellums among his friends. This was the first time in my life that I was directly involved in a mayoral campaign. After the signatures were collected, Joshua, my 18-month-old son and I, along with 1,000 other Oaklanders went to Laney College to present the signatures to Mr. Dellums and ask him to run. Mr. Dellums then consulted his wife, and they agreed that he would run for Mayor of Oakland. We all heard him say that, "If Ron Dellums running for mayor gives you hope, then let's get on with it." Those in attendance represented every aspect of the Oakland community: multiracial, intergenerational, multilingual and economically diverse. This was the city of Oakland at its best. Mr. Dellums' political history and leadership style meant if he won the election, that we, the people, would no longer be shut out of City Hall. We now could see the light at the end of the tunnel. The task that lay before us was getting him elected.

Ronald V. Dellums, like me, was raised in Oakland. For him to come out of retirement after serving 27 years in Congress and run for mayor was exhilarating. One of our own was willing to take the helm of the city. His candidacy invigorated people who had not been active in city politics since the Black Panther Party walked the streets. During his campaign, Mr. Dellums talked about Oakland as being the Model City and wanting to revitalize democracy. This became his mantra and we, his supporters, became the embodiment of it. We echoed it everywhere we went. I was hooked. I phone banked, organized meet and greets, and walked the precinct where Dellums was raised on Election Day. Mr. Dellums was elected mayor of the City of Oakland in June of 2006.

Dellums wanted all Oaklanders to know that they had a seat at the decision-making table and that their voices would be heard. He opened the doors of City Hall to Oakland residents and called for our collective genius to identify solutions to our own problems. This was my chance to have a 1960s political activist moment. Now that Dellums was elected, the real work was to begin.

As part of his transition into office, he called for the formation of several task-forces to address what residents considered the most pressing issues in the city. Instead of hiring outside consultants and soliciting "experts," he called for Oaklanders to create solutions to the problems they identified. Over 900 people served on 41 community taskforces. Of the 41 task forces, 8 were focused on education. I served as co-convener of the taskforce for creating enough teachers for Oakland youngsters and dealing with the impact of high-stakes testing.

The Effective Teachers for Oakland task force was formed to develop and implement recommendations to address the teacher shortage in the public schools and to ensure that all Oakland youngsters have effective teachers. Specifically, this taskforce was charged with answering the following questions: How can Oakland ensure that there are enough teachers for all Oakland youngsters? What is the impact of high-stakes testing on Oakland youngsters? As a group we focused more energy on the first question. In the initial phase of convening, each group met once a week for 6 weeks. At the end of the first 6 weeks each task force presented Mayor Dellums with 3 to 5 recommendations that would serve as his platform during his tenure. This process was one clear example of revitalizing democracy in the city. Because the task force recommendations became the mayor's political platform, all city staffers were aware of them and instructed to help with them. City Hall was becoming more open and accessible to the rank-and-file Oaklander.

One of the recommendations was to create an Oakland Teacher Center on behalf of Oakland youngsters. The Oakland Teacher Center was to recruit and retain teachers. The Teacher Center would be able to guide any Oakland resident on the path to becoming a teacher. The focus of the Center was to effectively solve the teacher shortage in the public schools by creating a local, permanent, and diverse teaching force for Oakland schools. We recognized that in the Oakland Unified School District, 50% of the teachers have European American monolingual mono-cultural backgrounds while 94% of the students have racially, ethnically and linguistically diverse backgrounds. We were also aware that due to No Child Left Behind federal legislation, school districts had to have" highly qualified" teachers in every classroom on the first day of school. To adhere to this mandate, OUSD, like many urban school districts, began to rely on national recruiting organizations like the New Teacher Project and Teach for America. However, many of the teachers they place leave the classroom after they have fulfilled their two-year commitment. Others leave to be near their families. These programs believe that the districts they recruit for have vacancies because the students are hard to teach and hard to reach.

However, in Oakland, we chose to frame this issue another way. We knew local citizens who reflected the diversity of the student population wanted to become teachers. So, this task force examined the structural barriers to becoming a teacher in California. We looked at how the requirements for becoming a teacher are prohibitive for local racially and linguistically diverse residents who want to teach in Oakland public schools and proposed a center to provide solutions. The following center departments were proposed: recruitment, test preparation, test fee assistance and retention. Our main goal was to employ the collaborative leadership style of Mayor Dellums and the power of his office to engage a cross-section of stakeholders in creating the center. There were specific things we did to move our idea forward.

On August 17, 2007, we held a teacher recruitment summit at City Hall. Task force members organized this event by developing cross-sector relationships and partnerships. Over 250 people came to City Hall that day to find out how they could teach in the Oakland Unified School District. The school district had principals, human resource professionals, and senior administrative staff on hand to do on-the-spot teacher and substitute teacher interviews. Holy Names University provided financial aid professionals to tell participants how they might pay for teaching credentials. The school district provided credential analysts to talk about credentialing requirements. The Learning to Teach Foundation provided six test fee reimbursement vouchers to be raffled off. Bake Sale Betty's donated pastries and locally owned small businesses made donations. Mayor Dellums and I addressed the attendees and encouraged them to become teachers, because a Model City has teachers from its own community. The use of City Hall for this event was vital here. We were beginning to feel a sense of ownership and responsibility for this municipal space.

While we did not get a physical space for the Oakland Teacher Center, the elements of the center became a school district program called Teach Tomorrow in Oakland. I serve on the steering committee for the program. During the second year of Dellums's term, Dr. Chris Knaus, associate professor of education at California State University, East Bay' approached Dr. Kitty Kelly Epstein, the Director of Education for the city about helping us with this program. We obtained funding to provide test preparation, test fee reimbursement, classroom support and professional development for the intern teachers in the Teach Tomorrow in Oakland

Program, who would become qualified, culturally diverse, educators who will live in and are dedicated to the community and will commit to teaching in Oakland's high-needs schools for at least five years.

One of the hallmarks of the multiple initiatives undertaken during the Dellums administration was to leverage the good work already being done in Oakland. This spirit of collaboration infused those who participated in the task force process. In 2009, I presented on the effective teachers for Oakland taskforce at the Hawaii International Education Conference. One of the attendees was Nyeisha Dewitt, a doctoral candidate at the University of San Francisco. She and I had met a few years earlier and had lost touch. She came to my presentation because, as an Oakland native who was living in a Bay Area suburb, she was deeply committed to improving educational conditions in Oakland. After the presentation, she was able to share an idea with me that we were eventually able to bring to fruition. Nyeisha and two of her friends, Dee Dee Abdur Rahim and Tamika Foster, wanted to have a Back to School Rally and Backpack Give-a-Way for Oakland students. All three women are Oakland natives and were in the process of creating a non-profit called Oakland Natives Give Back.

Over the next six months, meetings were held in City Hall to plan for the Back to School Rally and Backpack Give-a-Way. Although Oakland Natives Give Back took the lead in organizing, the event had several sponsors and partners. Capitalizing on the relationships created between the office of the mayor and the Oakland Unified School District, this would play a major role in getting students registered for school and ready for the first day. We were able to plug into the district's "Attend and Achieve" campaign that was starting in the fall to increase student attendance and student achievement. This event was broadly supported in the community.

The event took place on August 2009 at City Hall. There was something for everyone. High school students and middle school students had specially planned workshops. Parents were given information on how to make the school year more successful for their students. Kindergarten through fifth grade students had structured activities in the plaza that surrounded City Hall, Frank Ogawa Plaza. There were informational tables, face painting and jumpers. Scholastic Books brought Clifford the Big Red Dog. At the end of the day, over 1000 books had been given away. Pizza was donated by "The Pizza Man," Bay Area Fire Fighters provided water and other drinks, and the Alameda County Food Bank provided fresh summer fruit. There were speakers to motivate the community like former University of California Berkeley basketball player and Sacramento King player, Sharif Abdul Rahim and his friend, former University of California Berkeley basketball player, Oakland native, and world champion Boston Celtic, Leon Powe. Leon Powe graduated from an Oakland public high school and had had a difficult childhood and adolescence like many Oakland youngsters. He provided a motivational message about the importance of going to school and staying in school. The founders of Oakland Natives Give Back spoke about their joy in being able to give back to the city that had given them so much, and I addressed the crowd. My message was the task force's commitment to give Oakland students local, permanent, and diverse teachers. It was a wonderful day and a wonderful event. Not only were 1000 Scholastic books given away, but approximately 900 backpacks full of school supplies were also given away.

The event was a success. Many citizens marveled at their access to City Hall's bathroom, commenting that usually when such events were held at City Hall, they are made to use port- a - potties. The mayor was unable to attend this event, but several members of his staff were in attendance. Dellums did what he was elected to do and what he said he would do: he opened the doors of City Hall to the community, he trusted our genius to solve the problem we identified, and he stepped aside so we could implement our own solution. Ron Dellums chose to serve one term as mayor (2007–2010). In 2010, Jean Quan was elected as mayor of Oakland; however the legacy of the Dellums administration lives on. In 2011, we had the third Back to School Rally and Backpack Give-a-Way.

The rally and give-a-way build the momentum for students to go to school in Oakland and stay in school. The anticipated result of students going to school every day and doing their best work is that they will graduate from high school. Oakland, like many cities, is working to increase the high school graduation rate. While Dellums was mayor, Oakland was named a featured city of America's Promise Alliance thanks to Dellums's bipartisan relationships when he was in Congress.

Colin and Alma Powell founded America's Promise Alliance, a national collaborative effort to promise five things to the nation's students—caring adults, safe places, a healthy start, an effective education and opportunities to help others. The focus of the alliance is to increase the high school graduation rate to 90% by 2018 and guarantee that no school would have a lower rate than 80%. Oakland's Promise Alliance has a funded position to organize the local effort to increase the graduation rate. The membership of Oakland's Promise Alliance is comprised of representatives from the following: Oakland Alliance of Community Partnerships, LIBRE, Family and Student Engagement-All City Council (OUSD), Holy Names University, African American male achievement task force (OUSD), KQED, Assembly member Sandre' Swanson's office, Oakland Unified Police Department, Oakland Parents Together, Teach Tomorrow in Oakland (OUSD), Leadership

Excellence, McClymond High School Alumni Association, office of the mayor (Mayor Jean Quan), Imagine That, Oakland Housing Development, and Youth Council (City of Oakland). The members of the Promise Alliance harness the work that they are currently doing to increase the high school graduation rate. Using the collaborative style of the Dellums administration, this group shares resources, co-sponsors events and provides on-the-ground support to move initiatives forward. The Promise Alliance is an example of how we have institutionalized local genius and revitalizing democracy. Our program coordinator position has been funded for two consecutive years and continues to have an office in City Hall with the Quan administration. We are effectively transitioning our programs and initiatives into the priorities of Mayor Quan and her staff.

Reclaiming City Hall for the citizens in Oakland means two things. The first aspect is claiming the space of City Hall and using it to move community initiatives forward. It is about access, inclusion, and a sense of belonging. It is knowing what rooms are available and how to reserve them. And, more basic than that, it is about being able to simply use the bathroom in City Hall at a community event. The second aspect is a state of mind, the manifestation of operating in a true democracy where everyone is valued because of his/her humanity and everyone's voice is heard.

Mayor Dellums awakened a sleeping giant in Oakland. Long-time residents were re-energized, young people learned by doing and by consulting with wise elders. Large numbers of citizens were mobilized as in the time of the Black Panther Party. Young and old worked side by side on issues of importance to both. The bell of revitialized democracy has been rung. The 900 people like me who participated in the task force process have developed networks and new social capital. We have promulgated the area with our activism and continue to struggle for increased quality of life and equity in hiring practices on city construction sites. We continue to work in City Hall on the issues we have identified as important, and we continue to identify viable solutions to our own problems. Ronald V. Dellums and his administration illuminated something that my Grandma Doll knew. Cesar Chavez and Dolores Huerta knew it, too. Bobby Seal and Huey Newton knew it. Young activists like Jaron Epstein and David Nettles knew it. Those who organize students like Raquel Jimenez, Chantal Reynolds and Karina Najera knew it. Long-time activists like Ken Epstein, Geoffrey Pete, Henry Hitz and Alona Clifton knew it. Oaklanders like Nyeisha DeWitt, Joseph Lynch and Kwame Nitoto knew it and Alice Walker wrote it, "We are the ones that we've been waiting for." We thank Ronald and Cynthia Dellums for reminding us of this. The real work began by the people of Oakland in 2006 continues. This is the Dellums legacy, and we, the people of Oakland, reclaimed City Hall for ourselves, made it our own, and refuse to give it back.

H. Volunteers for the Mayor's Toy Drive fill City Hall

Endnote

1. Dr. Mayfield Lynch is a lifelong Oakland resident, the chair of the Education Department at Holy Names University, and the convener of one of Mayor-elect Dellums task forces, the Effective Teachers for Oakland Task Force

12

The Oakland Experience and What Academics Call "Participatory Action Research"

Most of the policies discussed in the preceding chapters were proposed by Oakland's participatory action process, the task forces.

Sometimes academics act as though coining a term is the same as creating a process. "Systems thinking' is a twentieth-century term but the concepts were discussed by indigenous people quite a few centuries ago. "Action research" was coined by Kurt Lewin in the 1940s but explained and used by a lot of European revolutionaries a hundred years earlier. Participatory action research has a similar dual reality. Sometimes it is planned by academics. However, the participation, analysis, and action steps of the action research cycle, now called "participatory action research," can also be used without the trappings of an academic endeavor. Orlando Fals-Borda describes several such cases in his book on participatory action in Latin America (Fals-Borda & Anisur Rahman 1991).

Participatory action research had a substantial community-based history in Oakland before the task force process began. It has been a major component of the youth organizing carried out by such groups as Leadership Excellence and DaTown Researchers (for web sites see appendices). The West Oakland residents discussed in the chapter on the Port also used this process to research and remediate environmental pollution. Some of the initiators were embedded in academic institutions; some were not.

I worked with Cynthia Dellums, VaShone Huff, Diane Boyd, Trina Barton and a dozen volunteers to pull together the first phase of Oakland's thousand member task force process which ultimately involved 46 groups. After the first round of task forces, residents requested others: entertainment; financing the city; and sexually exploited minors were three of these. People wanted to research, act, reevaluate and act again on particular issues, but they wanted to do these things to change their communities, not as part of a "research project." My history as both an educator and an organizer contributed to my sense of what would work. I speculate in this chapter that much broader use of participatory action can occur.

Universities themselves have struggled with action research as a concept and a practice. Patricia McIntyre describes an incident, only twenty years past, when she met with her dissertation committee to discuss her painstakingly developed proposal. She expected one member of her committee, a reputed feminist, to be supportive of the action research study on which she proposed to embark. That faculty member threw Patricia's paper on the table and said scathingly, "If you want to do research, do research. If you want to organize, then go do activist work." Poor Patricia sobbed in the bathroom afterwards, wondering how she could have been so foolish as to think her passion for knowledge and her passion for social justice could be combined into a project acceptable to an academic institution (McIntyre 2007). Other authors contend that universities have created a variety of conditions which are contrary to effective action research. These reservations and restrictions may be precisely the reason urban communities are a bit suspicious of things which have a university stamp on them. Sometimes university projects spend lots of money and do little. Other times the researchers seem constrained by bureaucracy and paperwork or unwilling to stand up for community actions when these might challenge their own reputations. And sometimes the projects just seem too small—always a pilot; never the big deal that is needed.

Alice McIntyre (2007) explains variants on participatory action like this: "Participant generated actions can range from changing public policy to making recommendations to government agencies, to making informal changes that benefit the community to organizing an event to simply increasing awareness about an issue native to the locale." The task forces did all these things.

In the terminology of academic action research, many of the groups have experienced several action research cycles. Here is one example: Recognizing that lack of employment is critically related to violence, the youth violence task force recommended the creation of 5000 jobs for youth, with 500 being created immediately. They also proposed "healing circles" for those experiencing violence in the communities and other activities for youth. Immediately after they made their recommendations, Mayor Dellums expanded his summer jobs program, created the Green Job Corps to increase the number of youth jobs, and prioritized job development within the context of the city's economic development strategy.

Task force members initially pursued funding for the healing circles with only small success, but when Oscar Grant was killed by a BART officer, members of the youth violence task force regrouped, reanalyzed, and pushed the issue again. Healing circles were held all over the city, some of them facilitated by task force members, and cosponsored by the Parks Department and community-based organizations.

Three years after the first phase of the task force process officially ended and several months after Dellums left office, the youth violence task force regrouped again to host a Nanotech conference in the packed Council Chambers of City Hall. Because they believed that Oakland youth needed an expanded vision of emerging jobs in science, Kweli and Chinyere Tutashina, Nina Horne and others brought hundreds of Oakland youngsters to hear sophisticated presentations and demonstrations by U.C. Berkeley nanotech specialists and other experts. Similarly, the OaklandWORKS coalition is an outgrowth of the Hire Oakland task force, and the effort has grown continuously for five years.

In addition to helping the task forces make their initial presentations to the mayor and, in the case of the education task forces, to the school board, I helped them to act as independent community groups pursuing their own recommendations to the extent that they wished to do so. I believe the task force accomplishments, as detailed in earlier chapters, have been impressive: a critical and long-awaited industrial land use policy, a new and much stronger local hire policy, a small business assistance center, new policies and programs on re-entry and other public safety issues which coincided and probably contributed to a large reduction in the rate of serious crime, funding of drop-out prevention work, an innovative approach to gang reduction through career pathways, a new program to create and retain a diverse group of effective teachers, new Port policies, a different mix of individuals appointed to important boards and commissions, an Office of Sustainability, and internet wiring of the recreation centers, to name just a few.

And because the task force recommendations remain in the public domain, they are a "gift that keeps on giving." (You can find them at www.oacp.net, the website of the Oakland Alliance of Community Partnerships) Holy Names University has, for example, started an "early admit" program which exactly mirrors the recommendation of the middle and high school task force, led by Jeff Dillon and Moyra Contreras, about how to create a college-going culture. Holy Names is sending "admit" letters to all the ninth graders at six Oakland public high schools as a way to make college a more attainable goal. The letter specifies the needed course and GPA requirements and removes the requirement to take the SAT or ACT exams. The impetus for this initiative was Holy Names' new president, Bill Hynes, but he reached out to a member of his own faculty, Kimberly Mayfield, who had been part of the task force process, to help with the details. Now Jeff, a school district recruiter and Moyra, a principal, are also being invited to help with additional advice.

For more information on some of the projects listed here, see the website listing at the end of the book.

There was no university involvement in the task force process. I do not say this to discourage university involvement. I am simply stating a fact and suggesting the option to other communities. I (and other members of the task forces) knew how to search for documents, compile a notebook of important material and chair meetings—all useful skills that are sometimes taught in a university. And a number of academics participated, among them Robin Freeman from Merritt College; Elnora Webb, who became the president of Laney College; long-time college teacher and activist Toni Cook; and Kimberly Mayfield Lynch, whose chapter is included in this book. However, no single "researcher" or "group of researchers" was necessary to carry out the process, and, to be honest, I think a university might well have been in the way. Our decision to do the process was instantaneous, and if we had needed to wait for a university to concur or disagree, our plans could not have been carried out before the mayor took office. I have related the process in some detail, including in the appendices, in order to encourage other communities to try something similar, with or without university involvement.

In the next chapter, journalist J. Douglas Allen-Taylor relates different aspects of Oakland's activism, its move to ranked-choice voting and the interesting result of the first election using this system.

13

Electoral Innovation:

Instant Run off Voting and the Election of the First Asian American Woman Mayor in the U.S.

J. Douglas Allen-Taylor[1]

Campaigns for major American political offices—generally begin in earnest some two years before the actual balloting takes place. When the 2010 campaign for mayor of Oakland began sometime near the beginning of 2009, many observers anticipated a heavyweight battle between the incumbent and progressive icon, Ron Dellums, and the powerful, ward-politics-savvy outgoing president of the California State Senate, Don Perata. Instead Oakland, with an Asian American population of some 16.84% (Oakland was 34.53% white, 28.02% African American, and 25.35% Hispanic/Latino in 2010), elected the first Asian American woman mayor in the U.S., Jean Quan. She defeated Perata after exhausting the full eight rounds of elimination balloting election procedure new to Oakland, ranked-choice voting (RCV), which is also known as instant runoff voting (IRV). While the 2010 mayoral race was the first election in which Oakland implemented RCV, the system has been in place in nearby San Francisco for several campaign seasons.

The contending candidates reflected the diversity of what many citizens boast is the most diverse city in the United States. Quan had been a radical activist in the '60s Asian American student movement at nearby UC Berkeley, evolved into a parent activist in the Oakland public schools, and was elected to the Oakland School Board and then to the Oakland City Council—specializing in budget issues, espousing the progressive beliefs that are key in most Oakland elections.

Perata, who was of Italian American heritage, began his career as a progressive (in an era when they were more often called "liberals") and climbed the elected ranks from the county board of supervisors to the state assembly and then to the pinnacle of the state senate. During that time he built a power base of ward politics from which he controlled or influenced many elected officials and government contracts in the East Bay, skirting ethical laws along the way and eventually leading to a five-year corruption investigation by the federal government. The federal investigation, although widely reported in area and state media, was quietly dropped a year before the Oakland mayoral election without any charges being brought against Perata. As is normal in such investigations, federal officials declined to release any details of their findings. Aside from the outgoing Dellums—who began his elective career in the mid-1960s in nearby Berkeley—Perata was arguably the best-known local politician in Oakland.

As is so often the case in city politics, Quan and Perata shared a long political history. Quan began her elected political career as one of the "Peratistas" (Gammon 2004), the widely used name given to Perata's officeholding protégés by the late *Oakland Tribune* columnist Peggy Stinnett; Quan later broke with Perata over undisclosed issues.

Two other top contenders in the race were City Council member and Democrat Rebecca Kaplan, a Jewish progressive and a former Green Party member seeking to be Oakland's first openly gay mayor, and Joe Tuman, a political science and law professor of Middle Eastern ancestry, a political commentator, and the only major candidate in the field without office holding experience.

Significantly, despite the fact that African Americans constitute slightly over 28% of the Oakland population, the second largest racial-ethnic percentage in the city, no black candidate was one of the top contenders (three minor African American candidates ran). This was the first time that no major African American had contended for the top Oakland seat since 1973, when Black Panther chairperson Bobby Seale ran a surprising second in the race against the incumbent mayor. Three of the last four Oakland mayors have been black. However, the lack of a major black candidate did not necessarily indicate a decline of black political influence in the city. African American political leaders and activists did not sit out the election, and each of the four top contenders—Quan, Perata, Kaplan, and Tuman—had significant and prominent black support in their camps.

In all, ten candidates contended for the Oakland mayor's seat in 2010. In the initial round of RCV balloting, Perata led with 33.8% of the vote, followed by Quan (24.53%), Kaplan (21.62%), and Tuman (12.02%). No other candidate came close to double-digit percentages in the initial balloting. After all but the top two contenders were eliminated in the subsequent eight rounds of balloting, Quan won with 50.96% over Perata's 49.04%.

Immediately following Quan's election, the Chinese international and Chinese American press celebrated the Chinese American's electoral victory as a victory for Chinese-descendant people in particular and Asian descendants in general.

Quan referred to herself as the "first woman mayor of Oakland" and "first Asian American woman mayor of a major American city" in her campaign brochures and added those descriptions in some of her stump and acceptance speeches. She told a post-election rally on the Oakland City Hall steps, "We've been waiting 158 years to have a woman mayor. We've been waiting over 200 years to have an Asian American woman as mayor of a major American city" ("Jean Quan Becomes," 2010).

However, this "historic aspect" did not appear to play a major role in the 2010 Oakland mayoral race. Asian Americans and women had been building their political power in Oakland for years, and the city as a whole seemed to look at the election of a woman and an Asian American, at some point, as inevitable.

Oakland voters have been electing women to major public positions since the 1970s, including the city's most recent representative to the United States Congress, as well as to the California state assembly, the county board of supervisors, the city school board, and the elected body in every area. In fact, men are now a distinct minority on the Oakland City Council, with six of the eight Council seats currently held by women.

Meanwhile, Oakland had been electing Asian Americans to its At Large City Council seat since the 1970s, breaking that trend only when Kaplan was elected in 2008. An Asian American woman served three terms in the state assembly from Oakland in the 1990s, and Asian-Americans have recently represented single-member districts on both the City Council and the Oakland school board. Quan herself was elected first to the school board and then the City Council, despite the fact that her Fourth District did not include Oakland's largest Asian American population concentration: Chinatown. And in none of these elections in which Oakland elected Asian American officeholders did Asian Americans represent even a plurality of the population, much less a majority. In such an atmosphere, the election of a woman and an Asian American as Oakland mayor would seem to have been only a matter of time.

The rise of Asian American political power in Oakland is even more notable given the divisions within the Asian American community. All ethnic and racial groups divide along political, social, economic, and age lines, but Oakland's Asian American population is also divided into four distinct national or regional groups—

Chinese American, Korean American, Japanese American, and Southeast Asian Americans. In addition, the Southeast Asian community is divided again into distinct nationalities of origin—Vietnamese, Laotian, and Cambodian. These nationalities often have distinctly different and competing economic, neighborhood, and ideological agendas.

Instead of racial or gender issues, Oakland's 2010 mayoral election focused almost entirely on the personalities and records of the candidates, the manner in which the major contenders ran their campaigns, and on the city's newly-implemented election system of ranked-choice voting.

Two issues predominated in the campaign. The first issue, in the midst of an epidemic of street violence, was the decision by the Oakland City Council—Quan included—in the summer of 2010 to lay off 80 Oakland police officers in order to close a major city budget gap. The second was Perata's campaign-spending practices in the mayoral election.

"Blue Skies and Opportunity"

The 2010 election took its final shape in August, when Mayor Dellums announced he was not running for re-election. All the major contenders—Quan, Perata, and Kaplan—had already announced but a Dellums candidacy would have significantly and unpredictably altered the race. For instance, Kaplan had won the support of a significant group of Dellums' supporters by indicating she would drop out of the race if Dellums opted to run.

Once Dellums was out, Perata instantly became the presumed front-runner because of the long reach of his Oakland-based political organization, his extensive name recognition based on his long years of political activity, and his formidable ability to raise campaign funds.

In a May 2007 article on Perata, the *East Bay Express* concluded that "few in state politics rival [Perata] as a fund-raiser," noting that the then-state senator had collected "at least" $3.72 million for his reelection campaigns between 2000 and 2006, and an additional $37.31 million was "raised by more than a dozen political action committees [Perata has] been associated with during that period" (Gammon 2007).

When federal law enforcement officials ended their five-year investigation of Perata in May of 2009 without bringing any charges, long-time Perata booster Chip Johnson, the East Bay political columnist for the *San Francisco Chronicle*, wrote that "with the dark cloud of a lingering federal probe behind him, there is nothing standing between former state Sen. Don Perata and the Oakland mayor's office but time, opportunity and blue skies" (Johnson 2009). Johnson's words reflected the extreme optimism—some might call it hubris—of the Perata camp.

Oakland's campaign expenditure limit law ($379,000 for 2010 mayoral candidates) should have neutralized Perata's fund-raising advantage. However, by exploiting a loophole in the law, Perata maneuvered to get the spending limit eliminated for this election altogether, and the Perata official campaign organization ended up spending $978,000 on the election. Two other organizations—the California prison guard-backed Coalition for a Safer California and the Oakland Jobs PAC—spent $233,000 and $76,500, respectively, in support of the Perata campaign, making the total amount spent in favor of Perata more than a million dollars. By contrast, Quan spent $380,408, Kaplan, $203,638, and Tuman, $79,155. Perata's campaign committee alone outspent the combined total of his three main opponents by a three-to-two margin, $978,006 to $663,201, and outspent Quan alone by close to three to one.

But that wasn't Perata's only source of campaign cash. He had figured out another way to circumvent Oakland's campaign finance limits. In February 2010, the *East Bay Express* reported that Perata had begun organizing a state ballot initiative to finance cancer research—under the name of the Hope 2010 Fund—and charged that Perata had systematically been siphoning off the fund's assets to help finance his mayoral race, an action that—if true—was illegal under both Oakland ordinance and state election law (Gammon 2010a). The *Express* reported that the Hope 2010 Fund was also paying staff members who were actually working full time on Perata's mayoral campaign.

The *Express*'s "Cancer in the Mayor's Race" article eventually forced Perata to temporarily liquidate the Hope 2010 Fund by distributing the money to legitimate cancer organizations. Following the election, Perata revived Hope 2010 and is moving forward with a cancer-related measure tentatively scheduled to be placed on the 2012 statewide election ballots.

With this overflow of money from both legitimate and questionable sources, Perata was able to finance a large stable of campaign consultants and staffers as well as to fund a series of full-color campaign brochure mailers and a saturation of advertisements on several cable television stations. At one point in the summer of 2010, this author counted four separate Perata ads on ESPN within the space of an hour.

By contrast, Quan stayed within Oakland's original legal campaign spending limit of $379,000 as a textbook example of how progressive candidates can manage a successful, low-budget campaign against a well-financed opponent. Quan, a relentless person-to-person campaigner, countered Perata's financial advantage and initial name-recognition lead by running a campaign heavy on precinct walking, door-knocking, and house meetings. The *East Bay Express* reported that Quan's husband, Floyd Huen, and campaign aide James Vann spent nearly a year themselves covering nearly two-thirds of Oakland's precincts, walking an estimated 200 miles in the process (Gammon 2010b). Quan herself claimed—we have no reason to doubt her figures—that she participated in some 200 "house parties," ("Jean Quan Becomes" 2010) small, highly-effective affairs in which a neighborhood supporter typically invites a group of neighbors over to his house for an hour or two of conversation and questions and answers. One of Quan's opponents, Joe Tuman, afterwards paid respect to Quan's electioneering tenacity, telling the Black Christian Network that "every day I was in house meetings, booked solid from morning until 10 o'clock at night, and wherever I was, Jean was there, too" ("Jean Quan Becomes" 2010).

Besides outworking Perata, Quan outgeneraled him, as well. Instead of hiring consultants, her campaign brain trust was her family, husband Floyd (a local doctor, county hospital board member, and a former college student activist himself), and her two adult children. In addition, the Quan campaign relied upon an estimated army of 1,000 volunteers rather than paid staff (Gammon 2010b). With the resulting savings in money, Quan was able to match Perata in the crucial political mailers, including several in the all-important final days of the campaign.

But the Quan victory was also helped immeasurably by errors and omissions by the Perata campaign. Perata, in fact, appeared overburdened by his large stable of campaign consultants, who seemed, from the outside, to get in each other's way and were never able to develop a consistent campaign strategy.

Perata began the campaign, for example, with a series of well-attended community meetings spread out across Oakland—four in all—in which he engaged in extensive question-and-answer sessions with voters. One of the more effective themes he used in those meetings was an attack on an earlier City Council decision to extend the hours of enforcement for Oakland parking meters—effective both because the Council decision was widely unpopular and eventually had to be rescinded, and because his two most serious opponents, Quan and Kaplan, had voted for it. Unaccountably, Perata stopped holding the community meetings in late spring and, in addition, never returned to what seemed his potentially profitable parking meter issue once the campaign got into full swing.

Instead of campaign meetings or rallies, Perata organized a series of highly publicized events in which Perata campaign volunteers staged "clean-ups" in several depressed Oakland neighborhoods. In one such event centered near 85th Avenue in what is known as "Deep East Oakland," campaign workers with bright-colored "Perata for Mayor" t-shirts put out Perata campaign yard signs along a three-block stretch of International Boulevard—the main local commercial thoroughfare—and then spent the next couple of hours picking up trash. The volunteers failed to canvass the neighborhood with literature, however, and took the yard signs with them when they left. Two days later, the area was as trash-filled as ever, with no neighborhood campaign organization established.

Finally, Perata himself appeared to suffer some sort of physical breakdown during the campaign. One of Perata's strengths—in the past—had been his ability to communicate directly with voters, an almost uncanny talent for appearing both folksy and sympathetic-friendly yet possessed of deep insider-knowledge, like the next-door-neighbor whom you engage in conversation every morning and only learn is a retired military commander in the middle of a conversation on the war in Afghanistan.

While that talent was on display in Perata's spring community meetings, it disappeared by the beginning of the campaign debates in the fall and never reappeared. In fact, Perata's debate performances got especially poor marks for what appeared to be a lack of interest in the process. One news report noted that in one early debate, for example, Perata "showed little fight and was almost listless as he avoided saying much of anything of substance" (Elinson 2010). And after the *Oakland Tribune* devastated the Perata campaign by leaving his name off its list of three top choices for mayor (The *Tribune* recommended Kaplan, Tuman, and Quan in that order), a member of the editorial board that interviewed the candidates painted an even more devastating picture of Perata's performance during an interview. *Tribune* columnist Dave Newhouse (2010) reported that while Perata is "considered the front-runner . . . his attitude [during the *Tribune* endorsement interview] was that he already had won the election. Unlike the other three, he leaned back in his chair, offered vague answers, and was sometimes uninformed on city policy. He had to be corrected by council members Quan and Kaplan."

Perata missed so many campaign debates that a local anti-Perata website began keeping score, noting in late October, for example, that he had skipped six of the previous seven debates. One possible explanation for this behavior may that he became physically worn down by the campaign, appearing to suffer from chronic coughing and laryngitis late in the campaign. His debate absences became a major issue, particularly in a mayoral race in which one of the underlying issues was that the incumbent—Ron Dellums—had failed to meet consistently with constituents. Opposing candidates often mentioned his name along with his absences or else spoke about him as "the candidate who chose not to be here tonight."

Anybody but Perata

Perata found that he was not only battling his official individual electoral opponents in the campaign; he was also taking fire from a powerful, independent force called the "Anybody but Perata" (ABP) movement. Following the 2010 mayoral race, there was considerable confusion concerning the relationship between ranked-choice voting, the "Anybody but Perata" movement, Perata's defeat, and Quan's victory. Central to the confusion was the widespread belief that the "Anybody but Perata" movement was born out of strategies necessitated by RCV, and that the movement was the sole creation of the candidates. That view was summed up in the *San Francisco Examiner* when a reporter asserted that, "two candidates formed a partnership to defeat favorite Don Perata" (Garcia 2010). Although the writer did not name the candidates who reputedly formed a "partnership," presumably he meant Jean Quan and Rebecca Kaplan.

The reality, of course, was somewhat more complicated. "Anybody but . . ." is a staple of America politics, superseding ranked-choice voting by a couple of centuries. The "anybody but . . ." strategy most commonly occurs in presidential party primaries after one candidate takes a large lead after several primary elections. Supporters of opposing candidates sometimes coalesce around a single opposition candidate, not because they want that candidate to win the nomination but in the hopes of denying the front-running candidate enough votes to sew up the nomination.

Anybody but Perata was a natural strategy for the non-Perata candidates to adopt in the 2010 Oakland mayoral race. Perata was the presumed favorite and front-runner in the race and an extremely polarizing political figure. With Dellums choosing not to run for re-election and with Perata's long record influencing both state and Oakland policies, he functioned as the de facto incumbent in the race.

The adoption of an Anybody but Perata strategy by the three top-tier contenders below Perata was manifest in the fact that all of them, in announcing their suggestions for second and third-choice votes, left Perata off their list. There was only one moment in the campaign when that strategy reached a formal alliance, however brief. When Perata put forward his successful bid to eliminate Oakland's campaign spending limit in mid-September, Quan called a press conference to denounce the attempt, asking each of the remaining eight candidates to join with her at the press gathering. Five did in person, and the event—widely reported in the local news—helped to make Perata's campaign spending a major issue in the race. (See, for example, Burt (2010) and Wagstaff (2010).)

The "Anybody but Perata" slogan itself was not a product of any of the candidates but was coined by an independent group of Oakland political activists not formally affiliated with any of the campaigns. The group put up an "Anybody but Perata" website (http://www.notdon.org) in April of 2010, and until November, the website was a "one-stop shop" for articles published in other media, as well as independently produced content, all of which worked in some way against Perata's candidacy. The website relied heavily, for example, on investigative articles on Perata originally published by the *East Bay Express*, which had been on something of a crusade against Perata since the beginning of the five-year federal investigation into corruption charges against the politician. Many articles—as well as those in such publications as the *San Francisco Chronicle*, the *Oakland Tribune*, and the *Berkeley Daily Planet*—would have been difficult to find for novice web surfers were it not for this website. The website also included self-produced anti-Perata YouTube videos and "print" ads. It also produced some of its own independent reporting, breaking the news, for example, that Perata had proposed the dismantling of Oakland's public ethics commission and its citizen police review board at some of his campaign meetings as well as tracking Perata's record of missing mayoral debates, the only news outlet to do so.

The website provided a focus of opposition to Perata, so the candidates opposing Perata did not have to produce anti-Perata content themselves but could concentrate their resources on positive promotion of their own positions. Although all the opposing candidates benefited from the website, only one openly embraced it. In one of her campaign brochures on education issues, the Quan campaign referred voters to the website "to read the articles about Don Perata and the Oakland school takeover."

The organizers of the "Anybody but Perata" website chose, almost exclusively, to remain anonymous (the only named organizer was J. Douglas Allen-Taylor), not because they had anything to hide but because they felt that the inevitable political attacks that would ensue had their names become public would have distracted the anti-Perata effort. Although website organizers supported various candidates—Quan, Kaplan, and Tuman, in particular—none was an official representative of a campaign, and the "Anybody but Perata" website was a strictly independent effort.

How important was the website to the defeat of Don Perata? Some observers gave it some credit, including the local African American newspaper. The *Oakland Post* wrote that "one of the main reasons that Jean Quan was elected was Taylor's website raised public awareness of an extensive FBI investigation of Perata and media exposés over the years. The Internet site, www.notdon.org, reached many people, becoming at times the third site listed by Google in searches for Perata's name. Precinct walkers for Quan and Kaplan reported that information from the website was often mentioned as they went door-to-door" ("Jesse Allen-Taylor's Pen" 2010). The Quan campaign itself gave the website significant credit. However, the website's actual impact remains unquantifiable, and the question will probably be left up to historians to decide.

Ranked Choice Voting and the 2010 Election

Traditionally, Oakland elections had been run under the non-partisan runoff system in which a candidate had to get an absolute majority in the first round of voting in a multi-candidate field in order to win. If no such candidate emerged, the top two vote-getters in the preliminary election competed in a runoff election. But in 2006 under Measure O, Oakland voters approved instant-runoff Voting (IRV)—later known as ranked-choice voting (RCV)—that had long been promoted by "good government" and progressive organizations.

Ranked-choice voting eliminates the need for runoffs in elections where a candidate needs 50% plus one vote in order to be elected. (Generally, runoffs are used in non-partisan races, such as for City Councils and school boards as well as for party primaries. In partisan general election races, where candidates run as nominees of their respective parties, candidates only have to receive the most votes—whether a majority or not—in order to win.) Under RCV, voters are allowed to rank a number of the candidates by preference (in the Oakland mayoral race, voters were allowed to make first choice, second choice, and third choice selections). The lowest-performing candidate is eliminated with each successive round, and the votes for that candidate redistributed to their voters' next "choice." The counting continues until one candidate receives a majority of the vote.

"Good government" advocates and progressives favor RCV in part because the elimination of a runoff saves public money, and candidates with lesser amounts of cash have a better chance of winning, since they only have one round of campaigning to spend it on. In addition, RCV advocates say that the system gives ethnic minority voters a better chance at victory, and turnouts are higher since they can be held in November—when more people traditionally vote—rather than on the traditional spring or summer primary date. Finally, RCV advocates say the system tends to decrease "mudslinging" because candidates seeking second- or third-choice votes must be careful not to piss off voters supporting their opponents.

(For an extended discussion of the benefits of RCV, see, for example, "Opinion: Ranked Choice Voting Making a Difference in the Bay Area" Crosscurrents from

KALW News March 25, 2011 http://kalwnews.org/blogs/ericamu/2011/03/25-
/opinion-ranked-choice-voting-making-difference-the-bay-area_907762.html)

Because the new system was specifically designed to help candidates who had
less money or who started out with a less name recognition, Perata—who had the
most name recognition and the potential to raise the most money in the 2010
Oakland mayoral race—opposed the implementation of RCV when it came before
the City Council for final ratification. In November of 2009, Perata sent a letter
to the City Council (later released as an op-ed under his name) in which he gave
a myriad of reasons why RCV ought not to be implemented, implying, among
other things, that the system could be "gamed," that it was unfair to minority voters (African Americans in particular), that it was confusing to voters, that it
impinged upon "the right to vote" and was a "civil rights issue." Reflecting both
the fact that Perata's influence over City Council decisions had waned since the
height of the "Peratista" days as well as the fact that two of the Council members
were candidates themselves and felt that they would benefit from RCV implementation, the City Council voted to move forward with RCV for the mayor's race.
Later events, of course, would prove that Perata was entirely correct in seeing
RCV as a potential detriment to his campaign.

In most ways, RCV performed as advertised. Turnout for the November 2010
mayoral election was far higher than turnout for the June 2006 vote when Ron
Dellums was elected (122,268 voters participated in the 2010 mayoral election as
opposed to 83,891 in 2006). Because the top of the lineups in the two races was
strikingly similar (the well-known Perata and two sitting City Council members
in 2010, the well-known Dellums and two sitting City Council members in
2006), some of the increase in voter turnout can almost certainly be attributed to
the fact that the 2006 election was held in the traditionally lower-turnout June primary season, while the 2010 election was held in the traditionally higher-turnout
November general election season.

Because no candidate received more than 50% of the vote on the first ballot,
Oakland would have had to spend money on a runoff election if RCV had not been
in place. Quan won under RCV as an ethnic minority candidate who was outspent
by Perata by more than three to one, cases in which RCV was advertised to help.
However, given the success of previous Asian American candidates in Asian-
minority districts in Oakland (Quan herself), Quan's better management of her
campaign, and Perata's mistakes and his numerous negatives for many Oakland voters, it is impossible to say that the same result would not have occurred if the two
candidates had met in a runoff under the old system.

One of the great myths that came out of the 2010 mayoral race—first advanced by the Perata campaign itself in the immediate aftermath of their defeat—was that Perata did not fully understand or appreciate the changes needed to be made to campaign under RCV and that, if he had, the outcome would have been different. Perata himself told a television reporter immediately after the election but before the votes were counted, "I don't understand how ranked-choice voting works" (Kuruvila 2010b). And when Jean Quan pulled ahead in one of the rounds of voting after trailing in earlier rounds, the Perata campaign issued a written statement that read, in part, "We're unclear about Alameda County's processes and await a final and accurate count," adding that "[t]he mystery of Ranked Choice voting continues" (Kuruvila 2010a). And following his defeat, Perata told reporters "I didn't understand it [RCV] enough. I ran the way I normally would" (Kuruvila 2010c). Finally, Perata campaign consultant John Whitehurst said after the election that "Hindsight is always 20–20, and if I were to run the election again, I would've gone negative on Jean and negative on Rebecca the way that they went negative on Don" (Richman 2010).

There is little to suggest that the post-election Perata campaign complaints about lack of knowledge of RCV were anything more than an attempt to make excuses for a crushing defeat in an election they expected to win. Perata campaign manager John Whitehurst, who led the excuse game, is a long-time, respected political consultant based in San Francisco, where RCV has been in effect for several years. In addition, evidence from the campaign suggests that Perata did try to use RCV to his advantage. The Oakland Black Caucus and the *East Bay Express* charged that Perata financial supporters were also backing African American candidate Marcie Hodge, most likely in the hope that Hodge would draw out black first-choice voters who would then put Perata as their second choice. There were also suggestions that the Perata campaign might have formed an alliance with candidate Greg Harland, who began the campaign attacking Perata but then abruptly switched gears mid-stream, turned his attacks on Perata's two chief opponents—Quan and Kaplan—and encouraged his supporters to pick Perata as their second choice.

The suggestions of a campaign alliance with Hodge and Harland illustrate that even if Perata did, indeed, try to "work" RCV to his advantage, he was blocked by the "physics" of the election. Had Perata gotten all of the second or third choice votes of the voters who made either Hodge or Harland their first choice, his vote percentage would only have been 38.5% of the total, far short of the 50% plus one needed for victory. That is because both Hodge and Harland had low vote totals. In fact, had Perata obtained the second or third choice votes of all the voters who made the six lowest-performing candidates their first choice (Hodge, Candell, MacLeay, Harland, Young, and Fields)—a practical improbability bordering on the impossible—his vote percentage would have only climbed to 43%. Only by tapping heavily into the second- or third-choice votes of the candidate who came in fourth—Joe Tuman—would Perata have been able to get over the 50% hump.

But here is where the "physics" of the campaign worked against Perata. Tuman had no incentive to make an alliance with Perata against Quan and Kaplan. Tuman was trying to win, and in order to win, he had to eventually pass Perata in the vote totals. The *San Francisco Chronicle* reported Tuman in a mid-October article, "Oakland Foes Trying to Stop Don Perata," as saying that Tuman had "been telling supporters he would vote for himself, Kaplan and businessman Greg Harland, in that order" (Kuruvila 2010a), pointedly leaving Perata out of the list.

Thus, the "approaching the speed-of-light" type physics problem blocked Perata from making RCV alliances that would have put him over the top. The higher the vote total of the contender Perata wanted to make an alliance with, the less likely that contender was to make an alliance with Perata, assuming he or she were interested in winning themselves.

A second widely disseminated belief about the mayoral race was that Quan forged such an informal alliance with Kaplan. An article in the *Bay Citizen* analyzing Quan's victory noted, for example, that "Quan . . . approached third-place candidate Rebecca Kaplan during a pre-election Sierra Club forum to discuss campaign reciprocity, in which both candidates would encourage their respective supporters to rank each other as their second choice vote. Though both Quan and Kaplan have said there was no formal agreement between the two, the method paid off for Quan" (Fetini & Elmusa 2010).

Not only was there no formal or informal agreement between Quan and Kaplan to trade second choice vote recommendations, Kaplan never specifically urged her supporters to choose Quan second. Instead, at an October 14 forum, she urged her supporters to use their second choice for Tuman and their third for Quan (Kuruvila 2010a).

On the other hand, Quan was specific in endorsing Kaplan for second choice votes. In answer to a question about her second and third choices, Quan noted at an October 14 debate at the college preparatory school, "we're trying to get anybody other than Perata elected. I'm on record as supporting Kaplan as my second choice."

This did not reflect a "ganging up" on Perata, as the Perata campaign later charged, but rather the advancement of careful, well-thought-out strategies to victory by both the Quan and Kaplan campaigns. Both Quan and Kaplan's strategies depended upon keeping the vote total of Perata—the early front-runner—below 50% up and through the final round of counting. Meanwhile, presuming correctly that Perata and Quan were ahead of her in voter preference during the campaign, Kaplan had to be careful about not being too chummy with Quan, lest that lead to encouraging voters to make Quan their first choice on the theory that Quan might have a better chance of defeating Perata than Kaplan. On the other hand, Quan most likely assumed, again correctly, that the ranked-choice counting would come down to a last ballot between her and Perata. Therefore, she encouraged her supporters to make Kaplan their second choice, because this would presumably create a feeling of good will among Kaplan supporters, who would then be more likely to make Quan their second choice. That strategy apparently worked.

Meanwhile, a mid-summer campaign gambit by the Perata forces not only illustrated the difficulties Perata faced in navigating the RCV waters, but also opened him up to counterattack on the fund-raising issue.

With Oakland facing a major budget deficit and the powerful Police Officers Association (OPOA) union unwilling to compromise on police contributions to pensions to ease the problem, the City Council voted in late June to lay off 80 officers. A group largely financed by the statewide California Correctional Officers Association prison guards union—longtime Perata supporters—sent out a supposedly "independent" mailing to Oakland voters protesting the City Council action. The mailers named Council members Jean Quan and Rebecca Kaplan as two of the chief instigators behind what they called "the effort to weaken Oakland's public safety program."

Quan, in fact, was one of the Council members who supported the police layoffs, but Kaplan was not. Kaplan, in fact, argued forcibly against the layoffs, voted against them, and presented an alternate deficit-reducing plan that was rejected by the Council.

Kaplan's inclusion in the mailers showed a particular problem in the Perata camp in a ranked-choice campaign in that two opponents (Quan and Kaplan) had a credible chance at victory. If the greater Perata campaign—including the so-called independent outside groups—attacked Quan (who was presumably the second choice in the race), they might be able to block her from victory, but the votes Quan lost would not necessarily go to Perata; instead, they might easily go to Kaplan, who was presumed to be running third. The greater Perata camp, therefore, decided to go after both Quan and Kaplan simultaneously, which blunted the effect of the attacks, especially when Kaplan and others pointed out—repeatedly—that the correctional officers' brochures had been in error. The official brochures and mailers of the Perata campaign did not attack his opponents. That activity was reserved for so-called independent expenditure groups which were supporting Perata but were not officially aligned with his campaign. However, local reporters immediately tied those "independent expenditures" to Perata (Rayburn 2010).

While Perata was forced to divide his attacks against his chief opponents, Quan and Kaplan were able to concentrate theirs. The two Council members rarely criticized each other in public during the course of the campaign. In her campaign meetings, debate appearances, and campaign mailers, Quan hit hard at Perata, sending out first a brochure mailer that promoted her qualifications, then a mailer that criticized Perata. Some of Quan's mailers did both in the same brochure. And Kaplan—hoping that Perata and Quan would negate each other—attempted to keep above that particular debate, opting instead to almost exclusively promote her own qualifications. Again, these strategies were based upon the different needs of Quan and Kaplan in the race. Quan needed only to keep ahead of Kaplan and vault ahead of Perata. Kaplan had to move ahead of both Quan and Perata.

Conclusion

The Quan campaign demonstrated how a progressive candidate from a lower-percentage ethnic minority, with a considerable financial disadvantage, can win against a non-progressive, heavily financed opponent—mostly by making better use of her resources and waging a smarter political battle. In addition, Quan had significant help from a third force—the Anybody but Perata movement. But each political district—as well as each individual campaign—is distinctly different, and anyone drawing conclusions from these campaigns has to understand that they must be adapted to their own situation.

Endnote

1. J. Douglas Allen-Taylor is a novelist and award-winning journalist and political columnist. He has written extensively about political, social and racial issues in his native Oakland and operated the Anybody but Perata website during the 2010 mayoral election.

14

Three On-going Campaigns

"Remember this: We be many and they be few. Another world is not only possible; it is on its way. . . . On a quiet day, I can hear her breathing."
Indian author Arundhati Roy, at the World Social Forum in Porto Alegre, Brazil, 2003

Mayor helps Teach Tomorrow in Oakland recruit diverse teachers for Oakland
Graphic design credit - Lynette Neidhardt

Despite the economic downturn, the city's budget crisis, and ongoing issues of violence, Oakland has dramatically rejected its closest brush (as described in chapter 13) with the sort of machine politics that dominates many Eastern cities. In such machines one politician has enormous amounts of money with which he can influence the decisions of other policy makers. Sometimes he uses the money to support projects that affect their constituents. In other cases, he contributes large amounts of money to their campaigns. And, in a third scenario he may make it clear that he will use his money to run a candidate against a policy maker who does not go along with his agenda. This means that open decision-making is stifled, because huge numbers of people become frightened to oppose the machine. Some of those with large amounts of money to contribute are various developers and law enforcement entities such as the prison guards union.

The election of Dellums in 2006 and Quan in 2010 demonstrated that Oakland voters would choose a different option when a real one was offered. The huge Port expansion made possible by Army base development; the community-minded board and commission appointments of Mayor Dellums; the actions against foreclosure; the on-going activism of the task force members; the really exceptional youth-organizing of people like John Brumfeld, Raquel Jimenez, and Karrina Nijera are optimistic signs that overcoming machine politics can have a democratizing impact. And these combined with a new generation of young leaders like Lailan Huen, a staffer in Sandre Swanson's office; Marisol Lopez, Mayor Dellums's former chief of staff; Chantal Reynolds, active in the Young Democrats and Black Women Organized for Political Action; youth culture genius, Ise Lyfe; Saleem Shakir, organizer for Concerned Black Men; Raquel Jimenez, who leads the school district's youth development and family engagement efforts; socially conscious teachers like Julia Ibarra, Adjoa Middleton, and Marisol Nuno; Corrina Gould, a leader in the Native American community; and Nyeisha Dewitt who heads up the Oakland chapter of America's Promise, are individuals who have shown themselves able to hold a big vision for a peaceful and loving community while creating immediate reforms in the areas of their own responsibility.

The task force effort produced new coalitions working on projects that continue, and, in some cases, expand on, the conclusions and recommendations of the original groups. Some of these priority issues can be summarized as follows: a) crime reduction needs a more accountable, community-oriented, and trained police force; b) every proposal and expenditure for economic development should directly benefit the current residents; and c) school and community need to be integrated in multiple, complex ways to the benefit of both children and adults. Many actions are being taken by individuals and groups on these key issues. I discuss one of the on-going efforts to achieve each of these goals in the following sections.

On-going Action on Police Department Reform

Rashidah Grinage participated in the police issues task force, which proposed that some areas of police services should be "civilianized." That is, civilians should replace police for the intake of complaints against the police for two reasons: 1) it is less expensive for the city to employ civilians in roles that do not really require uniformed police; and 2) residents will be more likely to turn their complaints over to a civilian. It is easier for an individual who feels he has been abused by an officer to describe the events to someone who is not wearing a uniform. Given the history of police–community relations in Oakland, there can be little argument with that contention.

The Dellums administration agreed with the idea of civilianization, but then-City Administrator Dan Lindheim, to whom the recommendation was referred, pointed out that the salary savings would not be realized for a few years until there had been some police retirements. Initially, there would be a cost to hiring the new civilians. Rashidah argued for placing these costs into one of the federal grant requests being made by the Dellums administration. This occurred; funding was obtained for two of the intake positions. Partial victory!! Let's celebrate!

Rashidah is a very determined person though—not to be deterred by partial victories. So she and Mary Vail, another task force member, the community organization, PUEBLO, and others have continued working to see full civilianization achieved. In early 2009 the City Council passed a resolution directing the city administrator to prepare a plan for turning the intake of citizen's police complaints over to the Citizens Police Review Board (Id 2009). Other organizations and individuals spoke up for the proposals and called for widespread civilianization (Ferro 2011). In May of 2011 Rashidah was cheered by throngs at the City Council meeting as she pointed out passionately that the jobs of other city workers could be saved if the city were not paying unreasonable police costs to intake resident complaints. She engaged many people in a campaign to meet with council members and publicize the issue. In spite of an exceptionally difficult budget year, various council members included funding for the start-up of civilianization in their alternate budget proposals. Everyone realized that there would eventually be a cost saving but committing funds to the start-up was the major hurdle. On June 30, 2011, the City Council adopted a budget which included civilianization, and the enhanced civilianization process will begin in 2012. Readers who are interested in police accountability issues might want to follow information on the website of the organization, PUEBLO (http://www.peopleunited.org/).

On-going Action to Achieve Jobs for Black Workers

Dellums' vision of using the army base for Port logistics promises a project which will generate 8,000 jobs. However, it is never automatic that Oakland residents will actually get these jobs and, if recent history were to continue, very few of those jobs would go to African Americans. Only 5% of construction hours on city-funded projects went to African American journeymen in Oakland in recent years, in spite of the fact that nearly 30% of residents are African American. Lots of people can give long complicated explanations. One succinct explanation comes from Geoffrey Pete, vice-chair of the Oakland Black Caucus, who told a City Council hearing, "We were good enough to build the White House and the plantations when we were free labor, but now that it's a paying job, we're not good enough."

Members of the local hire task force (and others who read their report) launched an initiative to repair this disparity—OaklandWORKS, a coalition which is campaigning for a centrally operated "jobs center" that will have resident participation in the assignment of jobs and the monitoring of all aspects of the process. Saleem Shakir from Leadership Excellence, Robyn Hodges from the WOCAG (West Oakland Community Advisory Group), and Brian Beveridge from West Oakland Environmental Indicators Project represent the group on a City Hall committee that is negotiating a stronger community role. Other groups in the coalition include the Oakland Black Caucus, Black Women Organized for Political Action (BWOPA), Oakland Parents Together, Oakland Natives Give Back, PUEBLO, and the John George Democratic Club.

Oakland Works sees an independent role for the community, which asks the construction trades unions as well as contractors to create an industry that facilitates employment for all, including black workers. Studies of black unemployment show the inability of black workers to obtain jobs in higher-paid industries like construction is a major cause of both income and wealth gaps. This is, in my view, another case where the potential for progressive action is marred by failure to take account of the racial wealth gap. It can be disheartening to see white "progressive" organizations calling black organizers "anti-union" because they speak up against discriminatory policies that are defended by both construction unions and contractors. OaklandWORKS has made a good deal of progress, and the agreements achieved are included in Appendix Two.

On-going Action to Achieve Full Integration of Schools and Community: Teach Tomorrow in Oakland

The diversity-oriented school boards of the 1990s helped Oakland to have one of the most diverse teaching forces in the country by creating the Oakland Partnership Program (Epstein 2012). When the state took over the school district in 2003, diversity in hiring was not a goal, and the teaching staff became less diverse, with ever higher rates of turnover.

The wealth gap issues discussed earlier make it more difficult for Latino, Asian, American, Native American and African American people to become teachers. The unpaid year of student teaching required by traditional credential programs is a major barrier for families whose average net assets are one-twentieth those of whites. But employing diverse community residents as teachers is absolutely necessary for a just city (Epstein 2012). Teaching jobs are numerous, stable, and come with benefits. Being excluded from teaching and construction jobs negatively impacts the incomes of communities already facing historic patterns of discrimination. In addition, children are deprived of teachers who speak the language of their families and live in their neighborhoods. To have a full-service community school, the community needs its residents to be employed in the school.

As Kimberly Mayfield Lynch describes in Chapter 11, Teach Tomorrow in Oakland was a task force response to this need. It is both a specific program and an educational approach. Its underlying rationale is the idea that teachers, like children, are whole people, bringing not only academic knowledge but attitudes, relationships, and values to their jobs. Children need teachers who see their families at the park and the grocery store, are permanently employed in the schools, speak the languages of the neighborhood, and share some history. This approach makes Teach Tomorrow not just an isolated program but what should be every urban district's general approach to recruitment

National organizations have finally taken up the issue of teacher diversity. Rachelle Ard spoke at the Center for American Progress in November 2011. Asked for the hundredth time why there is a need for teacher diversity, she replied, "I think we should stop asking that question." We need teacher diversity because we need diversity in everything, she argued. We should stop acting like there is a choice between diversity and quality. They are the same thing.

Teach Tomorrow in Oakland is also expanding its mission to create teachers who are able to fully implement other aspects of the district's full-service strategy. They are experimenting with new approaches, such as involving students in the interviews of new teachers and, on a voluntary basis, in their evaluation. Teach Tomorrow in Oakland has a website, listed in the appendices, which describes their complete agenda.

15

Gentrification and the Racial Wealth Gap in a National Context

Alexandria is that cute little town near Reagan Airport in the D.C. area. Not the place I would have picked to look for major gentrification issues. But in the Chatham Square area, just north of Old Town, newer residents living in market-rate housing are complaining to the police about people in an area called the Berg, where the residents are primarily black. Residents of the Berg point out that crime has actually decreased dramatically in recent years and say the complaints are unfounded. Supporting the argument of those who live in the Berg are statistics indicating that crimes in the public housing tract decreased from 115 in 2008 to 73 in 2010, and in Chatham Square from 28 in 2008 to 12 in 2010. One hundred fifty black residents held a community meeting in July 2011 about the situation (Perkins 2011).

So what are the wealthier neighbors' complaints? Betina Duschauld, for example, says she saw a young man urinating out a window. Others say they should not have to pay for a private security guard, a step they took because they thought there was more crime, which is actually not the case. The more affluent people also do not feel comfortable about people congregating on the street (Perkins 2011).

Missing from this and most other accounts of gentrification is any mention of the racial wealth gap. The difference in wealth is accepted as a given, yet the complaints of the wealthy frequently rest on wealth-based realities, not simply communication differences. "Hanging" on the street may not be so much a "cultural" choice as a result of lack of air conditioning and big backyards. A garden with a barbeque and swimming pool to "hang in" is an option for some but not for others. The problem with gentrification is not the race of the people who live next door, but the fact that the problems of the original residents are likely to increase as they are forced out of their original neighborhoods when costs rise. It is the economic dimension of race, not the personal one, which is at the heart of gentrification's impact.

I quote a Bay Area blogger named Roobs at length because he provides a simple explanation of how an "improved" neighborhood forces residents out, using West Oakland as an example.

> For example, let's look at a neighborhood in the City of Oakland in the San Francisco Bay Area. The neighborhood of West Oakland has long been a traditionally African American neighborhood. For many years, it has also been a low-income neighborhood. During the housing boom of the early 2000s, developers were converting old factories and warehouses into trendy urban lofts as well as constructing entirely new condo projects. Many started to worry about the potential for gentrification—original residents being displaced by incoming young professionals. So how would critics have solved this? Here's a thought exercise: Critics will say they wanted to see West Oakland improve but to maintain its "character." Of course, the character of a neighborhood is defined by its residents. So to maintain the character is to maintain the residents. So let's keep all the residents here. After working it that all the original residents can stay, they now want to improve the neighborhood, so let's keep developing. We turn those abandoned warehouses into lofts, put a new coffee shop and don't forget the supermarket (which West Oakland desperately needs—I'm looking at you, Safeway). We also work to improve the streetscape: install trees, pretty medians and new street lighting. Now we have a beautiful neighborhood with all of its original residents. It is a win, if only briefly. Because of the way our property and market system work, West Oakland will now be considered a desirable neighborhood. Thus, properties will become more valuable and the cost of living will increase. New residents will still have maintained their previous levels of income because we never addressed their income as a factor in how we improve the neighborhood. But now that their property is worth more, their property taxes also increase. If they rent their home, then the landlord will likely raise the rent to compensate for the increase in property taxes he or she is now paying. So without any interference from "evil" developers and all the good intentions of gentrification critics, original residents can no longer afford to live in their new and nice homes. Ultimately, it wasn't the fact that new hipsters or yuppies moved into the neighborhood,

regardless of their income. People have the right to move wherever they want to, after all. It was the way in which our system of market and property values works that put the original residents out. You cannot decry all that is gentrification while still demanding that neighborhoods need to be physically improved. And this is what critics are ignoring (Roobs, 2011).

His logic about the mechanism is good. His conclusion seems to be: gentrification cannot really be avoided, because neighborhood improvement means increased market value, and therefore the only real answer would be raising the incomes of those who live in affected communities like West Oakland. I appreciate his difficulty in finding an answer. Next door Berkeley, considered one of the most progressive cities in the U.S., lost 20% of its African American population in the 2010 census, and this follows equally large decreases in the preceding 20 years.

Junious Williams of the Urban Strategies Council makes these important points in analyzing the decrease of African Americans in the Bay Area and Oakland, in particular, over the past decade: He points out that part of Oakland's appeal is its history of black culture and activism. He also notes that the common characterization of gentrification as involving the same families who left during the "white flight" era "moving back" is probably inaccurate. The real gentrifiers are more likely younger whites who are able to move from rental status to ownership (of both houses and condos) in Oakland at lower prices than they would have to pay elsewhere (Arnold 2010).

Yet gentrification is a subsidiary problem. If wealth were not so unevenly distributed and if that uneven distribution were not racially based, the coming and going of various residents would have far less significance. It is not really the race of the newcomers that bothers the existing residents, so much as the assumptions and demands of the newcomers based on their relative affluence.

Do residents Ever Successfully Oppose Gentrification?

The journal *Environment and Planning* carried a study describing a neighborhood in Chicago which successfully resisted development by causing developers to think that new residents would be physically intimidated (Wilson, Wouters & Grammenos 2004). Liberdade, a neighborhood of Afro-Brazilians in Salvador, Brazil, successfully encourages residents to stay in their homes to maintain the culture, the history, and the sense of belonging and purpose which have been developed there. In these cases the neighbors have organized themselves in two different ways to resist gentrification. Do city policies ever halt gentrification or is the blogger Roobs correct? Does everything a city does to "improve" a neighborhood lead to gentrification?

Because I argue that gentrification is really a result of the racial wealth gap, we must first ask whether there are policies that can change that.

Gentrification and the Racial Wealth Gap

The most recent study of the racial wealth gap, conducted by the Pew Research Center, indicates that the gap between the net assets of the median white family and the net assets of the median black family has risen to 20 to 1, and the gap between white and Latino families is now 18 to 1. The median white family has $113,149 in assets; the median Latino family has $6,325 in assets; and the median black family has assets of $5,667.00. The report asserts that a large portion of this gap is attributable to the housing bubble and bust which depressed the median assets of all ethnic groups but most dramatically altered those of black and Latino families (Kochhar, Fry & Taylor 2011). U.C. professor Sandra Smith notes that African Americans and Latinos were actively targeted to accept new lending instruments which ultimately led to a bust that was more devastating for them than white families.

Dramatic as this Pew study may be, the wealth gap has been enormous for the entire 25 years that it has been tracked.

Median Net Worth of Households, 1984 to 2009
in 2009 dollars

	1984	1988	1991	1993	1995		2004	2009
Median net worth								
Whites	$76,951	$75,403	$68,203	$67,327	$68,520		$111,313	$92,000
Hispanics	$9,660	$9,624	$8,209	$6,853	$10,139		$15,188	$6,325
Blacks	$6,679	$7,263	$7,071	$6,503	$9,885		$9,823	$4,900
Ratios								
White-to-Black	12	10	10	10	7		11	19
White-to-Hispanic	8	8	8	10	7		7	15

Sources: For 2009: Pew Research Center tabulations of Survey of Income and Program Participation data from the 2008 panel; for 1984 to 2004: various U.S. Census Bureau P-70 Current Population Reports

PEW RESEARCH CENTER

Taking Account of the Racial Wealth Gap

The Latino, African American, and Native American communities, and some parts of the Asian community face a set of realities of which white progressives are only dimly aware; many of those realities are rooted in the racial wealth gap. The factors which produce that gap are historic—slavery, sharecropping, Jim Crow, Westward expansion, the seizing of land from Indians and from Mexicans, inheritance policy, the failure either to fulfill the historic promise of 40 acres and a mule or the contemporary demand for reparations. It also involves current policies on taxation, housing, credit, immigration, minority business, affirmative action, local hire, education, and incarceration (Reich 2011).

The wealth gap is not just another issue. It impacts every aspect of the lives of most residents of the country's major cities. Items which seem miniscule to most whites can be earthshaking to others. Is there enough money to go to the laundromat so the kids will have clean clothes for school tomorrow? Are there any black people working on the multiple construction projects underway throughout the town? Are "minority" businesses participating in new development opportunities when the rules are so skewed toward those with huge assets? Are any African Americans being hired in the fancy new restaurants that are built downtown? Is there any place to party downtown or have all the clubs been "fined" and "policed" out of business because the owners of new developments express unhappiness to the police departments about having lots of non-affluent folks downtown? Must everybody in some neighborhoods use the high-fee check cashing place because banks have so many restrictions on opening an account? Dad, who is a day laborer, has to carry around his money in cash: Will he get home with it, or will he be robbed? Is there any place that sells fresh produce within five miles of the house? Do the police show up when they are called and how do they behave when they get there?

Will the boys in the family be affected by gang recruitment and gun violence because they have no other source of resources or protection? Do girl-children line the streets of a major boulevard waiting to be molested for a price? Did the car get impounded because the driver has no immigration papers and can't get a license? How can mom take an English class, so that she can talk with the kids' teachers, when the state took away the money that funds adult schools?

The biggest difference is the segregated networks of different people. Many whites, even those who are not especially affluent, are able to borrow a hundred dollars in a dire emergency because they are part of families and groups that have the few thousand dollars in the bank that constitute the wealth gap. A Latino may lose his car because no one in his family has the money to pay a parking ticket or a tow. A Vietnamese family may have the utilities turned off because there is no one from whom to borrow the money for an extra-high bill in the winter.

Is Affordable Housing the Answer to Gentrification?

And, with no accumulated assets, can the non-white residents afford even the 10% or 15% increase in housing costs which result from gradual gentrification of the neighborhood?

Many progressives pose affordable housing as the answer to gentrification. I am not convinced for these reasons: 1) given the income and wealth levels of most urban residents, the ONLY units for which most would qualify are those set aside as "affordable," and 2) the number of such units generally included in these agreements seems miniscule. Here are some examples:

1. The Community Benefits Agreement negotiated in 2005 for the Oak to Ninth development in Oakland included 465 affordable units out of a total of 3,100 units. The affordable units are set aside for those families earning under $50,000 per year ("low" and "very low" in the agreement), but Oakland's median income is $41,000 per year. So, by this definition, most Oakland residents have incomes which are "low" or "very low," and the ONLY units for which most Oakland residents would qualify are those 465. This is only 18% of the units. Who will be moving into the other 2,635? It will have to be mostly people who do not currently live in Oakland, because so few Oakland residents could afford them. This is not, then, a project which primarily benefits Oakland residents. It actually contributes to gentrification even after the negotiations for affordable housing (Oak to Ninth CBA 2006).

2. The Los Angeles community benefits agreement with Los Angeles World Airport included 209 units of affordable housing, a very small number (Baxamusa 2008).

3. New York enacted new legislation in 2008 referred to as "80/20,"which has resulted in the creation of 20% low-income units in high-end Manhattan buildings. The integration of the buildings seems real and the results are very positive for the lucky families. But note again—20% for those whose incomes are under the 50% median and 80% for those above. Is that how we have come to define justice? And is there any logical reason for arguing that these projects are halting gentrification?

If Current Approaches to Affordable Housing Are Not the Answer to Gentrification, Can the Racial Wealth Gap Itself Be Eliminated?

I think the unprecedented OVERALL wealth gap may be reduced somewhat over the next few years as a movement grows against "the 1%." And I think that, in the long term, the racial wealth gap will also be reduced because of two factors: 1) whites are becoming a more distinct minority, and other groups are unlikely to tolerate the current extreme monopolization of resources forever; and 2) the biggest cause for the wealth gap is inheritance: white families have money and pass it on to their white children. But increasingly white families are not having white children. The younger generation is mixing things up with their choice of mates. So grandpa is going to end up passing on his wealth to some multi-racial grandchildren who will have a network of aunts and uncles and cousins who are both white and non-white. Then, when families do what they always do—loan each other money, help a nephew go to college, let the younger brother rent an unused house—those family exchange benefits will go to a diversity of people. (Thank you to educator Fred Ellis for his insights on this last important point.)

On the more immediate policy front, measures to compensate for historic and current discrimination have been resisted by whites. By and large, the only policies that have been allowed to stand are some of those generated by the student movement of forty years ago which encouraged and supported "Third World" higher education. Even these benefits have been reduced recently. Furthermore, although education may increase income, it does not significantly change the wealth gap which is based primarily on inheritance. The U.S. has not decided to apologize for slavery yet; let alone compensate African Americans with some form of reparations.

Those studying the racial wealth gap have not offered much new in the way of solutions. Bank accounts for school children are a nice idea but a rather insulting one when proposed as a solution to a problem with huge societal causes, costs, and ramifications. If gentrification rests on the wealth gap, and the will to end the wealth gap does not already exist, the answer to gentrification for now may have to be those improvised actions discussed throughout the book, the open resistance practiced in Chicago, the community consciousness campaign practiced in Liberdade in Brazil, and the OaklandWorks campaign to force more local hiring.

To Whom Do Cities Belong?: The Many or the Few?

I host a regular radio program on education. I interviewed a sharp young Oakland organizer and artist, Jonathan Brumfeld, who helps high school students paint murals all over town. He says, "Just give me a wall. We can make something beautiful."

"Don't you need grant money . . . or something?" I ask.

"No," he says. "People will come and give us everything we need. Just give me a wall. We can make something beautiful."

I thought he just loved art; then he explained to me that murals fight gentrification; they mark a neighborhood with the people's culture and heroes. This is art that regular people make without money, with just their ideas and wisdom. He says that it establishes whose culture dominates the neighborhood.

16

Organizing to Change a City:

Revisiting the Tactics

Recruiting a mayoral candidate has several potential benefits. First, the social justice-oriented people in a city have an opportunity to evaluate the candidate on their own terms without the bombardment of competing electoral claims. Second, the recruitment process itself may give the candidate a leg up against the big-money candidate. Third, and perhaps most important, the recruitment coalition may identify a new basis of electoral unity.

The best candidate for egalitarian change will have these qualities: a) financial and political independence from big developers, police and prison guard associations, and Chambers of Commerce. (He or she will need to work with these groups, but they will also need to be able to say "No" to them); b) the ability to see the exciting potential of the city as well as its problems; c) the humility to actually listen to regular residents of every ethnicity and adopt their proposals; d) an understanding of racism in all its dimensions and the willingness to prioritize needs and demands by communities of color even when they sometimes conflict with other progressive constituencies; and e) a sense of humor and the ability to speak in a compelling way, so that residents can hear the message even over the noise of the mainstream media.

Community Policy Making

Activists in other cities might consider something like the task force process. I am generally a political optimist, but even I was somewhat surprised by how well this worked. I think people in the U.S. are eager for a place to exchange ideas with people they do not know, if they think it might lead to action, and all of the on-going campaigns described in the book have benefited from the new connections established through the task forces.

Here are some suggestions about making the process workable. (Detailed questions, rules of engagement, and implemented recommendations are contained in the appendices.)

1. An elected or appointed official needs to express the desire for such policy-making to give people the sense that some of it will be implemented.
2. This official needs to be a big thinker who actually values people's participation and not a micro-manager who will try to make all the recommendations fit his/her pre-existing political agenda.
3. A fancy consulting firm is not needed and probably not helpful. Have the logistics organized by some diverse grassroots people who love their city so much they are willing to do it without pay. Then, if you come up with a little money, pay the people who make the copies and do the other non-glamorous jobs. This does not mean that the effort should be shabby and disorganized. People should have comfortable rooms to meet in and helpers around to assist with their questions, but it should be "grassroots" enough that regular people do not feel pushed to the margins. The people who made the Oakland process go included Trina Barton, Henry Hitz, Jaron Epstein, VaShone Huff, Marisol Lopez, Victor Ochoa, Gene Hazzard, Diane Boyd and others.
4. The most disenfranchised groups should be over-represented in the leadership.
5. Ask a question to guide each of the small groups.
6. Limit the process to a few meetings; 5 to 7 seems like a good number.
7. Don't wait for money. It really works better as a volunteer effort.
8. Make the recommendations very well known. Put the results in a local newspaper. Put them on a website. Put bound copies in the local libraries. This will allow people to pursue them for years, even if many are not initially implemented.
9. Put out some sort of newsletter, so that people know when various items are being implemented.

10. Encourage people to pursue implementation of their own recommendations.

Defending Progressive Elected Officials

"Progressives" have a hard time defending their leaders once they are elected, especially if they are elected to executive positions. The U.S. is a very conservative country; therefore, the policies and budgets that any executive is required to enforce are conservative. And in some ways, the mayors have the least flexibility of all. Oakland has done well in defending its legislative leaders—those who make the laws. A bumper sticker about House member Barbara Lee started decorating many cars in Oakland after her historic vote as the only House member opposing George Bush's Afghanistan policy. It said "Barbara Lee speaks for me." Dellums received similar kudos when he made historic proposals on South Africa and health care in the U.S. Congress.

But legislation and execution are not the same. Proposing good policies is not the same as governing from a base of bad policies (created by previous elected officials) and doing it with no money. For example, few big-city mayors would have supported the legislation that resulted in hundreds of thousands of inmates being incarcerated for petty drug crimes and then being returned to the cities with no jobs and no money. These policies were primarily created by statewide conservative constituencies who did not have to live with the results. Big city mayors deal with the crises that come years later. Only the most observant resident knows that local elected officials have little flexibility in handling these enormous challenges.

This is where progressive community leadership is needed—to point out progress where it exists, praise the leaders who are able to create it, and form the coalitions to campaign against those who have actually caused the problem, often at the state and federal level. Geoffrey Pete did a lot to provide this community leadership during the Dellums administration, and so did Steve Lowe, Margaretta Lin, Lynette Neidhardt, Henry Hitz, Kimberly Mayfield, June Ko-Dial, and and a few others who worked hard trying to get past the generally negative attitude of much of the mainstream press toward Oakland, in general, and Dellums, in particular.

However, the progressive groups which were helpful at getting Dellums elected were not good at publicizing the considerable successes of the administration. No one expects groups to speak up in support of policies with which they disagree, but this was not the case, in general, with Dellums. Land use, local hire, job creation via the Port, policy change for re-entry of the formerly incarcerated, diverse commission appointments, and many other changes were policies they had extolled before Dellums made them happen. I cannot explain it. Many of the groups were relatively successful at communicating with the press when they were protesting, but they seemed struck by inertia when there was something to support. If a community decides to run a genuine path-breaker for office, groups and individuals need to sign on to the work of long-term communication before they begin the campaign, and they need to have some courage about carrying it out.

Community Protection of Street Protests

The country needs large, organized, purposeful street protests to move away from a war-based, oil-based, profit-driven economy. And violence occurs sometimes to demonstrations organized by the most pacifist of leaders with Cicero and Birmingham being two historic examples led by the very king of non-violent protests.

Recently protest organizers in other countries have argued that violence is sometimes initiated by people who oppose the protests rather than individuals who support them. Some demonstrators in Canada developed pretty good evidence that there were, in fact, police posing as protestors and inciting violence: "Protesters are accusing police of using undercover agents to provoke violent confrontations at the North American leaders' summit. Such accusations have been made before and after similar demonstrations, but this time the alleged *agents provocateurs* have been caught on camera"(Police Accused 2007). Others have found members of right-wing groups posing as left-wing protestors. I have no evidence that any of this has happened in Oakland, but I do know what happened in a recent set of California protests:

1. The family of Oscar Grant, the young man whose death at the hands of a BART police officer led to months of intense organizing, asked repeatedly that people protesting his shooting not carry out destruction of Oakland in Oscar's name. Grant's grandfather said, "Don't dishonor my grandson's death by coming out here and tearing up Oakland."

2. Out of 78 individuals arrested in the June 2010 protests in downtown Oakland, only 19 lived in Oakland. Why did the out-of-towners not organize the violence they advocated in the city they came from, especially in light of the wishes of Grant's family? Those from California could have chosen Berkeley, Redwood City, Walnut Creek, all places where BART (the offending institution in this case) also operates. One 26-year-old white

man advocating destruction came from Salt Lake City. Could he not find any racism there to protest?

3. Something about the style and demeanor of those from far-away places did not convey the outrage that many Oaklanders expressed at unjust police actions. They joined the protests after dark, wearing zipped-up hoodies with eye holes.

4. Websites calling themselves "anarchist" advocated destructive protest prior to the demonstrations. While I do not support anarchism as a political viewpoint, it has a legitimate political history, which does not generally support random violence, particularly in situations which would harm poor and working people.

There are times when protest organizers may request the support of individuals from unions or solidarity organizations in other cities. These are sometimes referred to as "outside agitators" by conservative opponents of the protests, but this is inaccurate. They are invited supporters of a local movement. However, that was not the case in Oakland. No one was invited to fly in from Middle America wearing a mask and throwing little bombs. Following the very unified 20,000 person protest at the Port, Occupy Oakland lost support because of what seems to residents to be meaningless violence sometimes started by people who identify themselves as protestors. If I were a billionaire trying to stop the Occupy movement, I would find those folks very, very conveniently useful. So who are these folks?

Whatever the answer to this question, the immediate solution lies in a long-term disciplined and organized peace-keeper group like the one Taggart organized during the Oscar Grant protests with the assistance of MutimaImani. It should include community leaders, trade union leaders, clergy, and youth, and do monthly training in non-violent tactics for the organization and protection of protesting crowds. It will need to be strong and courageous to act in a way that supports the protestors and still contains individuals like the folks with the masks.

17

Organizing to Change a City:

Taking Space

If you take something you don't need and keep it then you stole it from somebody else who's hungry, everything that you do is everything you are.

Shadia Mansour

The idea of "occupying" space and creating parallel communities did not begin with the Occupy Movement in 2011.

As capitalism developed, the Left throughout Europe believed that organizing would take place at the "point of production" (often a factory) and that the power that workers had over profit-making would help them create social transformation. It was true then and it is still true, in places that now include the new industrial powerhouse countries. But egalitarian social change has also found other forms—from slave rebellions in the Caribbean to peasants organizing in Vietnam to poor people occupying unused land and making it their own in Brazil. Movements have a lot of new forms in the 21st century—the throngs in the streets of Tunisia and Egypt, the Afro-Latino organizing efforts in Latin America, Occupy Wall Street, and emerging ways that young and old in the U.S. develop confidence and connection as they organize to make existence livable and meaningful without commodities being exchanged for money.

People in East Oakland have started something they call 'time banking." People in the neighborhood do not have much money, but they have needs that can be met by their neighbors. A person takes care of someone else's children for several hours and banks that time. She can use her time to request translation or fix-it services from a neighbor who has those skills. Arnold Perkins, former head of the Alameda County Health Department helped to organize this process and talks about how it helps people to meet their needs at the moment and to know each other well enough to make some demands on City Hall when that is needed.

In Chinatown, hundreds of people have taken over a park, with no one's sanction, in the early morning hours to practice tai-chi.

Employees of the Parks department and Kijiji Grows are creating free gardens in every neighborhood, so that people can grow their own food. This is not just another "green" project. It is a necessity, because there is no fresh produce for sale in many neighborhoods.

The Oakland Black Caucus and Word Assembly have for several years treated every hungry person who showed up to a delicious and beautifully presented meal on most major holidays using only donations from folks who have only a bit more resources than those being served.

The creators of the turf-dancing phenomenon, another unique Oakland invention, help youngsters heal themselves with a highly structured, no-cost, and very physical set of maneuvers on a big floor. The term itself is an acronym for "taking up room on the floor" (Zamora 2007).

I conducted a radio interview which led me to investigate the international manifestations of this phenomenon. I talked with filmmaker Ben Watkins, who, with his wife, made a movie about parallel institutions that lead and develop communities in Brazil. These "quilombos," are named for the communities set up by escaped slaves. They provide for children, and sometimes adults, what the system often does not provide—education, discipline, physical health, recreation, and sometimes food. They are often centered in an art form—capoeira, drumming, circus arts, or something else. Ben explained that he found Brazilians proud and confident because they have maintained their history and art. At one point he called their oppositional community-making an "escape valve."

Then I visited Brazil myself. In Liberdade, a section of the city of Salvador, the 70,000 Afro-Brazilians who live there resist gentrification by intense encouragement not to move out of the neighborhood (personal communication, Roberto Merces). A large portion of Salvador was first settled by "squatting," which means that families took over unused buildings or land and improved them. People invite others over on the evening or weekend for good food and a project, such as putting on a new roof. And the incentive to stay in the neighborhood is a wonderful cultural atmosphere in which the daily burdens of racism are healed by the sense of community at home.

Ile Aye, located within Liberdade, is an amazing institution built around the yearly festival of Carnival and the educational needs of Afro-Brazilian youngsters. Most Americans have heard of Carnival and assume, I believe, that it is simply a party on a very grand scale. But the founders of Ile Aye have turned it into something more by developing a curriculum in black education which they expand each year through concentration on a particular theme. One year the whole community learned about the heroes of U.S. black history—James Earl Jones, Malcolm X, Martin Luther King. The education is carried on throughout the year, and on the day of Carnival 20,000 Afro-descendant Brazilians gather in the streets of Liberdade to celebrate Carnival together.

In Brazil, as in the U.S., there is both formal and informal, legal and extralegal "space-taking" on the part of marginalized people. While rural people are creating their own towns, the movement has also succeeded in electing a president and initiating reforms which have significantly altered their condition.

Brazil has adopted affirmative action and specifies that 30% of university slots must go to Brazilians of African descent. Populist President Lula initiated a policy whereby each family beneath a specified income level receives approximately $100 per month for each child who attends school regularly. And President Lula also succeeded in initiating a stipend for older people, regardless of their work history.

Argentinians Take Space

Nearby, in Argentina, workers have taken over factories that closed down in the wake of their 2001 economic downturn (http://communityrenewal.ca/i4 gateway004-breach). With nowhere to work, people occupied plants, fixed them up and reopened them. There are about 200 such factories, including Metal Varela, a foundry south of Buenos Aires, and they have seen a partial upturn in the Buenos Aires economy (McNair 2011).

Community Protection in Madrid

In Madrid multicultural communities have run the police away when they came to arrest immigrants from Africa. And the U.S. Occupy movement has many of its roots in Spain.

Improvisation in Bogota

Bogota, Colombia, has seen improvisation of a different sort with a humorous philosopher mayor who succeeded in reducing the homicide rate by 70%, traffic fatalities by 50% and provided drinking water to all homes. As an example of creative improvisation he hired 400 mimes to make fun of traffic violators, with apparently good success (Profile: Antanas Mockus 2010).

Protesters climb on big rigs stuck on the road after Occupy Oakland activists closed the Port of Oakland as part of a general strike in the California city on Nov. 2, 2011
(photo credit - Pamela Drake)

Occupy Wall Street . . . Occupy Oakland . . . Occupy Everywhere

This book goes to press as one of the largest movements ever to "take space" in the U.S. political imagination has set up tents in front of many of the nation's City Halls. At this moment in late 2011, 79% of Americans agree with Occupy Wall Street's key slogan: "The big banks got bailed out but the middle class got left behind" (Public Divided 2011). Although I have heard the critique that Occupy started without an adequate "program" or "demands," they seem to me the perfect example of the sort of improvisational action required when the traditional institutions have stopped working effectively for justice. As neither the Democratic Party nor the AFL can claim to speak loudly on behalf of the 99%, claiming a public space for a mass discussion seems like a good idea.

The General Assembly (mass meeting) I attended in front of Oakland City Hall was well constructed for a combination of mass involvement, movement education, and planning for action. Previous actions of Occupy Oakland were summarized; the 2,000 attendees broke into groups of ten for a brief discussion of "privilege"; there was a 20-minute forum on how "privilege" manifested itself in Occupy Oakland with each speaker limited to one minute; the Native American community proposed a resolution that was adopted, and then the planned November 2011 General Strike was discussed.

The movement has now been endorsed by dozens of unions and quite a few Democratic Party officials. It is changing the national conversation and providing some organizing experience to a new generation; that is all we can say for certain at this moment. But in Oakland it has raised again an issue which runs throughout this book: What do we mean by progressive? The Oakland police attacked a peaceful protest and sent an Iraq veteran to the hospital with a fractured skull. Oakland became the center of news coverage for a big part of the third week of Occupy, and commentators called for Mayor Quan to resign while locals asked if "progressive" was really an appropriate description of her. In my view, Oakland is better off with Ms. Quan, in spite of this and some other mistakes, than we would have been with the machine politics of Don Perata. It may be, however, that this new movement will bring new leaders with a better definition of "progressive" or a different terminology altogether, and the fact that these protests are taking place in the heart of the major cities may mean that the issues discussed in this book will become part of a far wider debate.

I am not counterposing what I have referred to as "taking space" with the actions I have described elsewhere in this book. I think the election campaigns, the participatory policy making, and the traditional demonstrations all have powerful impacts. I also think that people doing for themselves; taking over land not being used productively by large landowners, creating art forms, growing food in a park, developing institutions for their children, and taking over the banks and City Halls are another part of social transformation, contributing to the development of organizations that can also demand egalitarian and just local and national governments.

18

Organizing to Change a City:

Strategic Necessities

I propose here eight strategic elements that are important to the struggle for a just city when that city is relatively large and diverse. None of these factors will compensate for federal policies which favor the wealthy, encourage crime, and starve cities. Drug murders and foreclosures will probably continue even if progress is made on all of these local elements, because only national transformation is likely to reduce gun availability, the market for drugs, or bankers' control of the economy.

The factors I identify here are created by a whole community, not necessarily by city government. Ranked-choice voting, for example, was brought about in Oakland by members of the League of Women Voters and other community-based organizations, not by city government. And the achievement of each element is always incomplete, because every city is in dynamic flux, and none is isolated from the reach of international capital, state intervention, new pressure from developers or new federal mandates. Nevertheless I think this is a useful exercise.

The first strategic element is increasing political representation and involvement by eliminating the anti-democratic "reforms" initiated by the growth coalitions of the early 20th century. They were built on the elitist idea that the residents could not handle direct representation; Oakland has taken partial steps toward dismantling these anti-democratic structures. It has returned to a stronger mayor which means that the electorate can directly elect the person who wields the most power. The Council has instituted good but incomplete campaign finance limits which can restrain the unlimited influence of growth coalition money on election results, and Oakland has essentially returned to November city elections which ensure a higher turnout. Oakland has not reinstituted "partisan" elections in the sense of identifying candidates as Republican or Democrat, but this would not be especially helpful in a city where almost everyone is a registered Democrat. Instead Oakland has adopted the potentially more effective ranked-choice voting which seems, based on one election cycle, to encourage a stronger focus on the issues, leadership development of numerous candidates, and the ultimate victory of a candidate who is closer to the majority's views. (See chapter 13 for more details.) The trick with this election system will be the ability of those elected to pursue the full capacity of the progressive coalition by reaching out to the constituencies and leaders who supported another progressive candidate as their first choice. It remains to be seen whether Oakland's first candidate elected by this system, Mayor Jean Quan, will prove willing and able to do this.

The second strategic factor is creating an economy that does not depend primarily on high-end residential development. A big city with many low-income residents has to create an economy that is based on production and services. The Port provides that basis for Oakland. Many cities will be gentrified or become even more impoverished if they do not create such an economic base. This will involve constructing a very savvy multi-racial, progressive coalition which encourages investment without allowing business to run the political agenda. According to Domhoff's analysis, Santa Cruz has been able to do this, but few bigger cities have achieved that goal. I have cited Mayor Dellums' decision to focus on Port logistics as an example.

The third factor is assertion of political authority by those groups who together represent the ethnic majority in many cities. One of the most effective local struggles of the late 1960s was the San Francisco State Strike, a student campaign in which Latino, black, and Asian students organized separately; then created a coalition—the Third World Liberation Front—around common demands and finally invited friendly white faculty and student organizations to join them. Many of the racial justice reforms in higher education—more open admission, financial aid, ethnic studies, and others—can be directly traced to that strike and the one at City College of New York (Ryan 2010). A similar model is worth considering in cities where the economic needs of specific communities are being ignored by the growth coalition and City Hall. A broad program of critical issues developed in the Latino community would overlap in many respects with a program developed by Asian, African American, and indigenous activists. The employment of local diverse residents in teaching, for example, affects all these communities.

The fourth factor is a clearly defined program. In Oakland, big steps were made in creating such a program through the community task force recommendations. These reports consolidated in one place a surprisingly strong consensus of resident views on many issues.

The fifth factor is full control of the police force by elected civilian leadership. Oakland came closer to achieving this during the Dellums administration than it has come in recent memory. Previously the Oakland Police Officers Association had absolute control over hours of work and amounts of overtime to the detriment of public safety and city finances. Dellums changed this situation to some extent by insisting on a contract that put the chief in charge of assigning officers and limited unnecessary police overtime. Requiring officers to work on Saturday night instead of Monday afternoon definitely helps with the crime rate!

Previous city officials had been fearful of standing up to the OPOA. It was part of Dellums's mantra that he was "too old to be intimidated." Disrespect shown to Dellums at the funeral of several slain officers was widely interpreted as revenge for his effective stance against the Police Association's unreasonable approach to police staffing and overuse of overtime. Well-known Bay Area attorney, John Burris, communicated in a publicly distributed letter: "At a time that called out for healing, the OPOA chose to use their powers to stick in a dagger of retribution against the mayor, and that has left our grief unmitigated, and the reputation of this city tarnished" (Burris, J., personal communication, March 31, 2009).

In spite of his best efforts, however, Mayor Dellums was not able to completely institutionalize this stronger civilian control. As of this writing, the police chief hired by Dellums, Anthony Batts, has resigned, and the department is faced with a possible takeover by the federal courts. Judge Thelton Henderson has repeatedly expressed his dissatisfaction and at times outrage with the failure of the department to comply with the negotiated agreement that followed the "Riders" case involving resident abuse and police corruption. The court has noted, in particular, that the department fails to discipline its most out-of-control officers. Police behavior during Occupy Oakland in October 2011 could be another indication that Oakland has not achieved full civilian control. In addition, the role of the federal government in suppression of the "Occupy" encampments has led some to conclude that we have already lost much local civilian control.

Factor six is support for the development of individual neighborhoods. Oakland talks a lot about this, but the fact that most of the city's effort is organized around safety councils is a big drawback. A more general community organizing approach is needed so that people can get to know each for purposes ranging from baby-sitting, to book clubs, holiday parties, block parties and other interests. And preventing crime can and will be one result. But the current crime prevention councils are often not representative of the full demographic of the neighborhood. Excellent recommendations on broader neighborhood organizing were made by the neighborhood organizing task force (www.oacp.net).

Seventh is a communication system which allows more progressive elected officials to communicate what they are doing and regular residents to communicate with each other. Oakland does not have this. The African American newspaper, the *Oakland Post*, is the best source of alternative perspectives. And there are individuals like long-time activist and former elected official, Alona Clifton, who keeps many people informed through her network. The cities identified as "progressive" by Domhoff are small, and one reason they are able to achieve "progressive" status may be that small size makes personal communication easier, so that residents are not overwhelmed by the blare of the mainstream press.

Factor eight is widespread personal initiative accompanied by the recognition that justice is negotiated day by day, street by street, school by school, and struggle by struggle. It is as much East Oakland time-banking, Brazilian squatter rights, and Libre youth development as it is City Hall policy making. There is a natural tendency to seek a neat boundary around the set of policies which will "make everything better." The national and international context means that is impossible. Recruiting a mayor, instituting ranked-choice voting, personal and group initiative to implement the task force recommendations, vibrant youth culture and mural movements are some of the many indications that Oakland residents tend to trust their own wisdom and initiative, no matter who resides in City Hall.

Our current period has no road map. We're going to have to embrace each other—from college students to mural artists to small business owners, unemployed immigration activists, and union strikers—if we're going to get from here to the world that Arundhati Roy can hear breathing.

Appendix One:
Documents of the Task Force Process

1. Some Implemented Task Force Recommendations

Many of the recommendations of the mayor-initiated community task forces have been implemented. Below is a small sample of such recommendations. (Complete task force summaries can be found in the task force section on the website of the Oakland Alliance of Community Partnerships (www.oacp.net) under the Task Force tab.

Economic Development Task Force Recommendations

1. The task forces recommended focusing economic development on growing sectors that will create quality jobs. This refocusing occurred: Port and logistics, health care, green jobs, restaurants, and small business development have all received attention.

2. The task forces proposed expanding access to banking services and financial education for the many Oaklanders who have no access to banking. Several financial education seminars have been held. The mayor, with other partners, developed "Bank on Oakland," which is providing bank accounts and other services.

3. The task forces recommended increasing "contract compliance" staffing which monitors the implementation of local hire policy, utilization of small businesses, and so on. This was done.

4. The task forces recommended a stronger local employment hiring policy. In 2010 the mayor directed the enforcement of a strict 50% local hire policy with no "core employee exemption."

5. The task forces proposed and assisted with the creation of a Business Assistance Center. This was supported by the mayor and Council; it opened and it has served 1,000 people thus far.

6. The task forces proposed an Office of Sustainable Development. This was created.

7. The task forces recommended "green workforce development." This has occurred with the creation of the local "green job corps," which has become a national model.

8. The task forces recommended the creation of an industrial land use policy. In 2008 the Council passed a modified version of Mayor Dellums's proposal with strong advocacy from the task forces, the Chamber of Commerce and several labor unions (Burt & Rayburn 2008).

9. The economic development task forces proposed appointment to the Port Commission of a resident of the communities that border the Port. West Oakland resident Margaret Gordon was appointed to the Port Commission.

10. Task forces proposed attention to the health impacts of Port activity. Many steps have been taken, including reduction in truck emissions by those trucks traveling to the Port through the City of Oakland.

11. Task forces proposed zoning the city. This happened.

12. Task forces recommended that appointments to boards and the commission be more economically and ethnically representative of the city. This has happened and is especially notable on the planning and Port commissions.

Education, LGBT, and Immigration Task Forces

1. The task force on effective teachers recommended that the city and school district hold teacher recruitment summits to provide Oakland with diverse, permanent, and local teachers. The mayor's office sponsored two such events at City Hall with a total attendance of over 400 individuals.

2. Teach Tomorrow in Oakland, the program created through collaboration of the mayor, effective teacher task force, school district, and teachers union has placed three cohorts of diverse, permanent, local teachers in the schools.

3. The task forces proposed remodeling the city's entire website to promote civic participation and transparency in government. This redesign occurred.

4. The task forces proposed the creation of "wrap-around" services for Oakland youngsters. A broad collaboration obtained $18 million for the creation of school-based health centers and family support centers. These are five middle school sites in addition to the high school health clinics which already existed. This makes Oakland one of the front runners in the country in terms of providing school-based health care. The sites are administered by Safe Passages.

5. They also proposed making the schools into centers of community and after-school activities. There has been a great expansion in after-school programs; the school board has initiated a "community schoolyards initiative," and the new superintendent has focused his strategy on "full-service community schools."

6. The task forces recommended that the school district be returned to local governance. The mayor supported this position and through the work of Assembly member Sandre Swanson and local residents, local control has now been returned.

7. The task forces proposed greater use of the Peralta Community College system to benefit all the residents. This has occurred with the development of numerous new programs including a "green jobs" program, a "gateway to college" program, involvement of Peralta in the Promise Neighborhoods planning and many other programs.

8. The task force on middle and high school students proposed a "youth advocate" program. Implementation of this was begun by the school district with the "Inside-Outside" Advocate Program and an expanded volunteer program.

9. The high school and higher education-related task force proposed expansive projects which would create a culture of learning in the city and provide opportunities for higher education and job training for every Oakland graduate.

   a. City Hall has hosted three back-to-school rallies; mentorship has vastly expanded; the district is now pursuing "multiple pathways" for every graduate.

b. A local college, Holy Names, has introduced an "early admit" program through which every 9th grader receives an acceptance letter to college contingent on completion of college prep courses.

10. The mayor's office, United Way, the school district, the teachers union; and America's Promise Alliance launched a comprehensive anti-dropout initiative with a conference of 300 people at Castlemont High School.

11. The literacy and technology task force proposed vastly increased access to the Internet. The task force helped Parks director of capital projects, Mark Hall, to wire all the recreation centers in the city. A letter from Mayor Dellums helped Oakland Technology West obtain more used computers for their on-going project to rebuild them and provide a computer to every Oakland student who requests one.

12. In response to the LGBT task force as well as state and national events, Mayor Dellums became one of the first in the country to perform marriage ceremonies for gay couples, including a number for the task force members themselves.

13. In response to issues raised by the immigration task force Mayor Dellums declared Oakland a sanctuary city and implemented a new police policy which would give drivers without licenses (often undocumented) time to have a relative pick up the car before it was towed, stored and sold, or destroyed because of inability of many residents to pay the high fees and fines.

Public Safety Task Force Recommendations

1. Declare every police officer a community policing officer (carried out by the mayor).

2. The task forces recommended that the mayor's office launch a citywide campaign to educate staff, police department, and ultimately the community about community policing and public safety. This began but has been stalled by budget cuts.

3. Convene meetings and mediations with Oakland's youth to seek insight in resolving issues of violence and crime and determine what youth need. Several have been held and new innovative initiatives are underway.

4. Retain Chief Tucker to ensure compliance with Riders' consent decree. This occurred. And now the Mayor has hired a new police chief who will also focus on these issues.

5. Strengthen Riders' consent decree by continuing the compliance period. This occurred.

6. Resolve Oakland Police Officers Association contract. This occurred.

7. A comprehensive master resource guidebook manual for those re-entering society from incarceration has been produced!

8. Clean Slate events (some have been held; others are underway).

9. Geographic assignment of officers in order to make community policing more workable.

10. Employment of a re-entry specialist in the mayor's office.

11. Obtaining the largest federal grant in the country in order to maintain employment for officers who would otherwise be laid off.

12. Banning the box that asks about felony arrests on city applications.

13. Obtaining funding for a "day reporting center" for individuals re-entering Oakland from incarceration.

2. Roles and Responsibilities of Task Force Conveners

(Developed by the Dellums transition team and National Community Development Institute (NCDI))

Each task force will address a defined question. For example, the task force on green industry will ask: "What city policies and actions could help to make Oakland a center for green industry?" The task force on housing will ask: "How can we see that Oakland residents at every income level have decent, affordable housing?"

1. Task force co-conveners will participate in an orientation session and will participate in additional orientation, debriefing, and collaboration sessions.

2. The task force co-conveners will work to create an atmosphere of vision, optimism, diversity, and inclusion.

3. The task force co-conveners will:

   a. Make arrangements for translation, child care and transportation, if needed;

   b. Prepare agendas for meetings using the six-session format as a guideline;

   c. Convene the meetings, ensuring democratic participation and the flow of each session, by asking members to raise their hands, keep their comments brief, and so on;

   d. Research needed information and ask other members to do the same;

e. Facilitate a consensus among members on policy recommendations;

f. Communicate with other task forces which are working on related issues; and

g. Communicate with members of the task force about needed information.

4. Assign two task force members to:

a. Record minutes and proposals on a laptop and

b. Serve as time keeper.

5. Periodically ask members for brief written evaluations of the process and attempt to use this information for constant improvement of the meetings. One such evaluation should be done at the end of the first task force session for the purpose of debriefing and planning.

6. Attend one neighbor-to-neighbor session and incorporate the information obtained into the deliberations of the task forces.

7. Remember and remind other members that the task force does not speak for Mr. Dellums.

8. Respect the process.

9. Attend one collaboration session with all conveners on September 30.

10. The planning process will last for approximately six–eight weeks. During that period co-conveners should be prepared to spend approximately eight hours per week preparing for meetings, researching policy recommendations, communicating with task force members and other conveners, evaluating the process, and so on.

11. Maintain sign-in sheets.

12. Read the report of the Dellums Commission, when it is issued in November.

13. Reconvene the task force after reviewing the Dellums Commission Report if necessary.

14. Turn in a final report by December 8. This report includes:
a. one to three-page statement of the advisory recommendations and community initiatives;
b. two or three pages of the most important back-up information and a binder with minutes and supporting documents. (Format will be provided for these.)

3. Working Agreements for Participants

1. Respect the process.
2. These are ADVISORY committees—Recommendations are not set in stone.
3. Patience.
4. Mutual respect.
5. Be open and inclusive. (Draw out everyone's opinions (full participation).
6. Don't attack other people's solutions.
7. Raise your hand to speak.
8. Conflicts/struggles will happen, but let's work towards solutions.
9. Follow the decision-making criteria and try to achieve consensus. If there is no consensus, there is the option to issue a minority report.
10. Make recommendations and provide steps to make them happen.
    a. List obstacles and challenges.
    b. Provide implementation steps.
11. Provide clear structure to enable effective and productive democracy.
12. Embrace and model a new vision for Oakland which includes:
    a. Reinvigorating democracy.
    b. Empowering residents.
    c. Living the Model City.
13. Take care of ourselves.
14. Celebrate our successes along the way.
15. Have fun.

4. Sample Questions Guiding Individual Task Forces

The 41 initial task forces were divided into issue groups (education, public safety, economic development, etc.). Each individual task force had a question or questions to guide its discussion. Each task force met on a specific night of the week. Below is a chart of Thursday evening task forces and the questions that guided their deliberations.

TASK FORCE GROUP	TASK FORCE NAME	QUESTION
City government	Planning, zoning, and land use	How can planning, zoning, and land use policies be most effective to enhance the lives of Oakland residents?
Diversity	Immigration	How can the city enhance the quality of life for immigrants?
Economic development	The Port	What policies will protect the health and environment of Oakland residents, while fully developing the economic potential of the Port:
		What relationship between the city and the Port will bring maximum benefit to the residents of Oakland?
		How can Oakland be enhanced as a center for world trade?
Economic development	Oakland as a center for multicultural arts initiatives	How can Oakland become an economic center for the multicultural arts?
Education and community learning	Local control	How can we return full local governance of the schools to the Oakland community?

Neighborhood organizing and civic participation	Neighborhood organizing and civic participation	How can we revitalize democracy through the organization of neighborhoods, enhancement of civic participation, and constituent services provided by the mayor's office?
Public safety	Police issues	What contract and policy provisions could create adequate public safety in all neighborhoods and employment of a larger number of Oakland residents as police?
Education and community learning	Creating enough teachers for all Oakland youngsters and dealing with the impact of high stakes testing	How can Oakland ensure that there are enough effective teachers for all Oakland youngsters? How can Oakland deal with the impact of high stakes testing on Oakland youngsters?

Appendix Two:
Sample Documents Demonstrating the Changing Approach to Economic Development

1. "Oakland OKs industrial land-use policy"

by Cecily Burt and Kelly Rayburn, Staff Writers (Burt & Rayburn 2008)

The Oakland City Council voted to protect hundreds of acres of industrially zoned land early Wednesday, but not before siding with developers who want to build housing in a heavily industrialized area of the Central Waterfront.

The 5–3 vote to approve Council member Nancy Nadel's land-use policy may have momentarily muffled the years-old argument over the fate of Oakland's rapidly shrinking supply of industrially zoned land, but there are still plenty of details to be worked out. Those details, such as coming up with criteria and conditions under which a housing development or other nonindustrial use might possibly be allowed in an industrial zone, are sure to reignite the debate.

The council's action came two weeks after Mayor Ron Dellums' office backed a policy to preserve all of Oakland's remaining industrial zones, which have been declining in size as residential developers buy up large, inexpensive parcels and obtain general plan amendments to build housing on the sites.

The trend of allowing new residential developments in historically industrialized areas of Oakland scared off some potential companies who worried about future complaints from new neighbors over noise or smells.

Dellums' proposal sought to reverse that by sending an unambiguous message that Oakland welcomes new businesses and they would no longer have to compete with developers for scarce industrial land.

A competing proposal presented at the same meeting by Council member Larry Reid (Elmhurst-East Oakland) would have done the opposite, critics charged, by changing the general plan to promote housing in several industrial areas, including his East Oakland district.

The council took no action on either one.

The hybrid approved Wednesday was offered by Nadel (Downtown-West Oakland). Nadel has been a fervent backer of preserving industrial land in her district, some of which has been purchased by developers in the hopes of getting it rezoned.

In order to preserve that land and to send businesses a message that Oakland welcomes new industrial opportunities, Nadel agreed to support Council President Ignacio De La Fuente's desire for splitting one industrial zone south of High Street in half to allow waterfront housing below Tidewater Avenue.

> "We reached a difficult compromise," Nadel said. "I'm pleased we can now move forward with attracting new businesses . . . and we have a lot of businesses that are looking for space. Our next step in West Oakland, on April 17, is to hold an economic development meeting to start presenting some of the business opportunities we hope to attract."

De La Fuente, meanwhile, scoffed at criticism from some that he and Nadel entered a behind-the-scenes agreement rather than looking out for what's best for Oakland as a whole.

"This is what it takes to move agendas," De La Fuente said. "Rhetoric won't get you anywhere."

De La Fuente and Nadel were joined in voting for the motion by Council members Henry Chang (at-large), Jane Brunner (North Oakland) and Jean Quan (Montclair-Laurel). Opposing the plan were Council members Desley Brooks (Eastmont-Seminary), Patricia Kernighan (Grand Lake-Chinatown) and Reid.

Reid opposed the Nadel proposal after the council voted down his attempt to change areas near the Pulte Homes Arcadia Park project in his district to residential zones. Both Reid and De La Fuente said some industrial areas have sat blighted for as many as 20 years and that the way to bring economic development is to consider new uses.

De La Fuente said it can be done in a way that protects current industrial operations.

"We are not eliminating one single job," he said. "There's not one area where we're pushing out one single company."

Dan Lindheim, the Community and Economic Development Agency director and a close adviser to Dellums, said that even though the council did not vote on the mayor's original proposal, the city took a significant step in protecting industrial areas.

"The result wasn't bad at all," he said. "It was actually quite good."

New housing isn't necessarily outlawed under Nadel's proposal. Developers could continue to apply for general plan amendments to allow residential projects in industrial zones, but those projects would have to meet strict criteria that will be developed by city staff.

The criteria, which will be formulated in the next two months, could include a range of factors such as whether a mixed-use buffer is needed between industries and residential areas.

"There is no consensus on what the criteria will say, but many of us will be asking for criteria that includes community benefits for anyone who wants to apply for a general plan amendment in any industrial area," Nadel said.

The vote to allow housing below Tidewater Avenue—home to Hanson Aggregates, a busy concrete and asphalt production plant that has trucks lined up three-deep most mornings waiting for loads, as well as White Bros. lumber mill—was not welcome news for some in the close-knit business community there.

Rich Bourdon, a majority owner of Design Workshops Inc., a custom woodworking and cabinet business on Lesser Street that would remain industrial under the council's new policy, said he doesn't feel safe.

Bourdon moved his business from San Francisco's Market neighborhood eight years ago because of market-rate loft housing residents who moved in nearby and complained about the noise and smells. At the city of Oakland's urging, he bought the building and put $2 million into it. The company has 100 union workers.

Now Bourdon is worried about another potential glut of new residential neighbors moving in and starting to complain about the noise from his dust blowers, the cement trucks blocking the street and who knows what else.

"That's our biggest concern in the neighborhood, that these businesses, even though they are grandfathered in, will be deemed nuisances and forced to leave," Bourdon said. "That was one of the major reasons we left San Francisco and came here, because they were putting residential all around us."

Scott Peterson of the Oakland Metropolitan Chamber of Commerce said the chamber has long urged the council to adopt criteria that would guide development and create buffers to protect industrial businesses, so he is gratified that it will now be done.

But giving up Tidewater shows the council's direction and message is not as clear as it could be, he said.

"The Chamber is committed to doing everything we can to communicate to businesses that Oakland is a good place to invest . . . and we have plenty of areas we can pay attention to, especially in West Oakland," Peterson said. "But the writing is on the wall in other areas. It's not the way to sustain the economy.

"We need a clear message: Here are the types of jobs we want, here are the types of jobs and skill levels, and here are the benefits to the community by attracting those jobs."

2. Oakland Army Base Community Benefits Agreement on Jobs, October 27, 2011

It dealt with city policy toward construction and operations jobs created by the Oakland Army base development, and passed the City Council in the Spring of 2012. Among these were individuals who had been members of the original Dellums task forces.

Local Hire (for Construction and Operational Jobs)
Past Areas of Agreement

- 50% (plus one) work hours for Oakland residents, craft by craft.
  There should be additional priority for local hire given to:
  1. West Oakland residents.
  2. Enterprise Zone residents (or another proxy for areas of low-income, high employment, etc. task force will further develop.)
- 100% of *new* apprentices must be Oakland residents.
- Unions/contractors must guarantee that Oakland journey workers will get preference.
- Existing workers in Oakland must be recruited for job opportunities.
- A study of existing trained workforce in Oakland is needed.

- Employers need to disclose info on jobs in advance (construction and operations).
- Contractors should get credit for local hire if they employ workers at other projects in other cities.
- Majority agree that there should be a one-source center for all employees.

TASK FORCE ISSUES	TASK FORCE AREAS OF AGREEMENT
• *Develop priority criteria for local hire*	• "Local" is defined as the City of Oakland, with priority being given to the zip codes that comprise West Oakland and City Council District 3, and then to all of the Oakland Enterprise Zone.
	• Staff will conduct a capacity study of West Oakland to better understand the skills, needs, and demographics of the targeted population.
• *Clarify hiring process at jobs center*	• The jobs center should be located in West Oakland, be readily accessible, and serve as a resource for contractors, employers and job seekers during construction and operations phases.
	• The center will connect job seekers with job training, education and other support services, such as transportation.
	• The center will be overseen and administered by an independent body. Staff will develop an RFP for the operations of the jobs center
	• To meet local hire goals, contractors would send requests to the union hiring hall and to the jobs center simultaneously. If the hall cannot provide a local worker within 72 hours, the contractor then would call the jobs center to provide a qualified worker. All such workers need to be dispatched through the appropriate union hiring hall.
	• The jobs center will monitor and track job assignments and worker hiring and retention. On a regular basis, the jobs center will transmit these results to the monitoring and enforcement sub-committee of the stakeholder oversight committee for compliance determination and enforcement actions.
• *Should Oakland residents who had to move away be included in the local hire policy? If so, how?*	• Not included in recommendations.

Training and Job Pathways
Past Areas of Agreement
Apprenticeships

- There should be a requirement for a specific number of *new* apprentices, craft by craft.
- There should be a number of apprenticeships set aside for graduates of pre-apprenticeship training programs.
- Statistics and regular reports on the number of pre-apprenticeship graduates in apprenticeships, and number of apprentices becoming journey-workers should be provided.
- Contractors should be required to keep apprentices on for at least one year, beyond that the requirement will be negotiated case by case.
- Need a mechanism to recognize, analyze and ensure that contractors use apprenticeship graduates on a long-term basis (must include an enforcement mechanism).
- Need to define and implement pre-apprenticeship training standards.
- Apprentices should reflect ethnic diversity of Oakland community.

General Workforce Development

- City/Community Economic Development/Workforce Investment Board should have a workforce development plan for the Army base. Community colleges should be encouraged to offer associate's degrees as well as certificates to trainees.
- Existingworkforce development/job training programs should be utilized to train workers.
- Use linkages with Peralta Community College district.
- Employers must provide advance information on the type of jobs, number of jobs, and duration of jobs.

TASK FORCE ISSUES	TASK FORCE AREAS OF AGREEMENT
• *Develop appropriate number for new apprenticeship requirement*	• The goal for the percent of overall apprentice work hours should be raised from 15% to 20% of total work hours. • 25% to 50% of apprentice hours worked must be worked by new apprentices. (This translates to 5% to 10% of total work hours). Task force did not reach agreement on exact number. • Developers/contractors will get credit for new apprenticeship hires once the apprentice has worked 1,000 hours. • New apprentices are defined as individuals who have not worked in union construction prior to being hired on the Oakland Army base (OAB) and who are starting at the entry level of a 1st period apprentice. • Stakeholders will contribute to a revolving loan fund that could help pay for initiation fees for low, very low, and extremely low-income new apprentices. • New apprenticeship hiring opportunities shall be given first to qualified graduates of Oakland pre-apprenticeship training programs. • Jobs center will track and support the progress of apprentices becoming journey-level workers. • The Oakland Workforce Investment Board (WIB) should take a lead role in establishing pre-apprenticeship training standards.

Young Adult/Re-Entry Employment Program
Past Areas of Agreement

- Need job training and placement opportunities for young adults (18 and over).
- For youth (under 18):
  - Start basic math and reading foundational skills training in middle schools.
  - Funding for high schools, like McClymonds and others, to offer pre-apprenticeship training for pathways to Army base jobs.
- For formerly incarcerated workers:
  - Require employers to ban the box on the job applications.
  - Jobs should be open to folks on parole or probation.
  - There should be a commitment by employers to hire re-entry workers.

      ° Employers cannot ask for credit references.

      ° If a background check is required, it should be done at the end of the hiring process.

- There should be targets set for hiring and retaining re-entry workers and other disadvantaged workers.
- There should be incentives/penalties associated with meeting re-entry/disadvantaged worker targets (i.e., discounts on lease payments).
- Need outreach and education to both employers and potential employees (young adult/formerly incarcerated).

TASK FORCE ISSUES	TASK FORCE AREAS OF AGREEMENT
• *Develop definition of "disadvantaged worker"*	• "Local Disadvantaged" will include such populations as low income young adults (18–25), disabled individuals, and the formerly incarcerated.
	• The jobs center will follow Federal Department of Labor guidelines for defining "disadvantaged." Under the Workforce Investment Act (WIA), the term ``disadvantaged adult'' means an adult who received an income, or is a member of a family that received a total family income, that, in relation to family size, does not exceed the higher of the poverty line or 70% percent of the lower living standard income level. Dislocated workers also qualify for support under WIA.
	• Formerly incarcerated residents also qualify as disadvantaged.

Monitoring and Compliance
Past Areas of Agreement

- The city, Port and community must all make a commitment to doing monitoring and compliance, including a commitment to funding staff to do monitoring and compliance.
- Resources are needed to train community members to participate in monitoring.

- A joint committee made up of representatives from the community, labor, government, and contractors should be responsible for the oversight of monitoring and compliance.
- A majority of the committee should be from community groups and should represent a cross section of the community.
- WOCAG should be part of the stakeholder oversight group.
- The committee will have the authority to recommend solutions and to enforce penalties when contractors are out of compliance.
- Majority support a "good faith" effort to reach goals.
- Tough penalties are needed to hold contractors responsible for meeting goals. There should be non-monetary penalties in addition to monetary penalties such as:
  o increase local hire percentage (as an option instead of withholding retainer funds), and
  o ban contractor from future Oakland work.
- Penalty funds should go towards training, one-stop job center, monitoring and compliance, and/or a fund to address other problems associated with meeting the local hire goals.
- There must be a process that includes technical support, to help contractors get into compliance.
- There should be incentives for contractors that exceed goals by 10% or more (and are on schedule).

Task Force Issues	Task Force Areas of Agreement
• Define the "good faith" hiring process.	• "Good faith" efforts will involve utilizing "name call," "rehire," or other similar programs at the hiring halls to reach goals when they are available as part of the hiring hall dispatch procedures, as well as using the jobs center as a resource if the union cannot provide the local residents as requested. • The oversight committee will review the "good faith" efforts of the contractor or employer and determine whether they meet the goals of the community jobs agreement, including local hiring and the city's local employment program goals. • If the committee determines that "good faith" has not met, then there may be penalties and referral to arbitration.
• What should be included in the monitoring program, e.g,. retention, verifying residency, software?	• The task force agreed on the need for an ongoing monitoring program, including the use of technology to register clients, ensure they meet the definition of "local" and track their retention.

• *What is the definition of "community" in terms of determining community representatives on stakeholder/ oversight group?*	• In general, membership would be composed of representatives from the local community, developers, labor, contractors, employers, the city and the Port. • No consensus on specific composition of committee or definition of "community."
• *Should this committee be modeled on the Port's social justice committee?*	• No consensus on this issue. • There should be a "transparent, participatory and stakeholder model" for the oversight committee. • Representatives to the stakeholder oversight committee would have to be specific individuals, committed to serve a term and to participate regularly. The task force members agreed that the stakeholder oversight committee should be a separate entity from the jobs center and its related advisory board.
• *Develop overall structure and general content of agreement (community workforce agreement, project labor agreement, etc.).* • *How can PLA meet the goals of community benefits?*	• A binding community jobs agreement (CJA) will serve as the overarching policy and program framework for construction and operations jobs. The terms of a PLA for the construction jobs must conform to the mutually agreed upon local hiring and program operations requirements within the CJA. • The CJA should be a "3rd party agreement" between the developers, the city and community stakeholders (representatives to be determined). A CJA would provide signatories with legally enforceable rights and obligations. • The terms and conditions of a project labor agreement, community jobs agreement and development agreements must be aligned and consistent. • A CJA should be developed and approved prior to the city of Oakland signing a PLA for the Army base development.

Project Labor Agreement
Operations Jobs/ Card Check
Past Areas of Agreement

- Need operations jobs for Oakland residents, including blue collar and white collar jobs.
- Need an additional focus on sustainable industries like clean energy, movement of agriculture products, clean energy, and recycling, and on green jobs.

- Want permanent jobs not temporary ones. If temporary workers are employed, there needs to be a time limit and there should be a pathway for temporary workers to become permanent.
- Seasonal workers ("casual workforce") can be hired directly by employers, but temp agencies should not be used.
- The majority wants a card check for all operations jobs, but there was no consensus.

TASK FORCE ISSUES	TASK FORCE AREAS OF AGREEMENT
	• All of the policies developed for local hire, disadvantaged workers, the CJA and the jobs center also apply to operations jobs. • The jobs task force did not address the implementation details of the operations phase jobs.

Appendix Three:
Some Relevant Websites

Asian/Pacific Islander Youth Promoting Advocacy and Leadership (AYPAL): http://www.aypal.org

Black Women Organized for Political Action (BWOPA): http://www.bwopa.org

Teach Tomorrow in Oakland: http://www.teachtomorrowinoakland.net/

Holy Names University Early Admit Program: http://www.hnu.edu/admissions/earlyAdmit.html

Intertribal Friendship House: http://www.ifhurbanrez.org/

Insight Center: http://www.insightcced.org/

Kijiji Gardens: http://www.kijijigrows.com/

Leadership Excellence: www.leadershipexcellence.org

National Community Development Institute: http://www.ncdinet.org/media/docs/2899_Spr08newsletter.pdf

Oakland's Latino History Project: http://museumca.org/LHP/

Oakland Alliance of Community Partnerships: http://www.oacp.org

Oakland Natives Give Back: http://www.oaklandnatives.org

Oakland Post News Group: http://content.postnewsgroup.com/

Oakland Technology Exchange West (OTX West): http://www.otxwest.org/

Oakland Business Assistance Center: http://www.oaklandbac.com/

Rhythmic Uprising: http://www.rhythmicuprising.org/film.php

Urban Fire: http://www.urbanfire.org

Urban Habitat: http://www.urbanhabitat.org

West Oakland Environmental Indicators Project: http://www.woeip.org

Appendix Four:
A Brief Oakland Timeline

1200 B.C.   Ohlone Indians settle in the area that was later named Oakland.

1772   Spanish explorers arrive in the East Bay.

1820   Luis Maria Peralta is awarded a 44,800-acre land grant from the king of Spain that includes most of present-day Alameda County.

1821   The first non-Native American dwelling in what is now Oakland is built by Antonio Maria Peralta near Paxton and 34th Streets.

1850   Oakland Chinatown begins with the arrival of Chinese immigrants, making it one of the oldest Chinatowns in North America. Many are driven from the gold fields by bigotry. More Chinese arrive to help construct the Central Pacific Railroad's western portion of the First Transcontinental Railroad. The Chinatown neighborhood in Oakland is a pan-Asian neighborhood.

1853   The College School (Henry Durant, principal) is established in a rented room on the corner of Fifth and Broadway. It will later become the College of California, predecessor to the University of California. The first public school opens with an attendance of 16. The Oakland Police Department is founded.

1864   County supervisors rent an Oakland house to serve as the first county hospital. The first street paving is laid in Oakland, on a small portion of Broadway at a cost of $3.18 per foot.

1867   The first Oakland black public school opens; then closes in 1871. Dr. Samuel Merritt donates 155 acres of dammed tidal water from the headwaters of Indian Slough. It becomes known as "Merritt's Lake" and later Lake Merritt.

1869   The first Oakland horse car runs from the estuary to 40th and Telegraph. Oakland becomes the western terminus of the Transcontinental Railroad as the first westbound train arrives on the Central Pacific railroad in the area now known as Old Oakland.

The Oakland Fire Department is established.

1870   Starting in the 1870s railroad employment becomes a major mechanism for African American movement to the East Bay. African Americans generally work as sleeping car porters.

1870   Mary J. Sanderson opens the "Brooklyn Colored School." Brooklyn was a separate town just east of Lake Merritt. Schools in Brooklyn and Oakland were integrated in 1872.

1870   Anti-Chinese sentiment is rampant in the 1870s in Oakland and elsewhere in California.

1872   The town of Brooklyn is annexed to Oakland.

1874   The federal government dredges the channel to open Oakland as a deep water port.

1886   Joaquin Miller, distinguished poet, purchases a site in the Oakland hills, naming it "The Heights." Miller plants some 75,000 trees on the 70 acres to create an artists' retreat where the mutual enjoyment of nature would nurture the creative spirit.

1890   The first black Baptist Church in Alameda County, Beth Eden Baptist, is founded. Its minister, Rev. Allen, later founded Allen Temple Baptist Church.

1891   Oakland's first electric streetcar leaves the foot of Broadway for Berkeley. Residents throng the sidewalks as if it were a parade.

1904   The first public recreation area, Bushrod Playground in North Oakland, is deeded to the City by Bushrod Washington James.

1908   First Women's Suffrage march in California is held in Oakland.

1909   The area of Oakland increases from 22.9 to 60.25 square miles with the annexation of Claremont, Fruitvale, Melrose, Fitchburg, Elmhurst, and other outlying territories.

Oakland's population more than doubles in ten years from 66,960 to over 150,000 as people and businesses relocate from earthquake-ravaged San Francisco. Oakland regains control of the long-lost waterfront by final settlement of litigation which had lasted over half a century and cost several million dollars.

1910–1920   The first barrio of Latino immigrants is established in West Oakland

1921   In August 1921, the Knights of the Ku Klux Klan, Inc. open an office in downtown Oakland, declaring that they intended to "keep a closer watch on public officials."

1922   On May 5, 1922, 1500 men in white robes and masks gathered in the Oakland hills to burn a fiery cross behind an American flag in an initiation ceremony for 500 new Ku Klux Klan recruits.

1925   C. L. Dellums helps establish the Brotherhood of Sleeping Car Porters, the first African American trade union in U.S. history. Dellums serves as the union's vice president and president. In 1995, Oakland's new train station is named the C. L. Dellums Amtrak Station.

1926   Charter amendments are adopted which create a permanent Port commission and transfer to the county the assessment of city property and the collection of city taxes. Moviegoers flock to the opening of the Grand Lake Theater and are thrilled by the sounds of its mighty Wurlitzer organ.

1927   With the organization of the board of Port commissioners, the municipal harbor enters a new era of development as the "Port of Oakland" including the opening of the 700-acre Oakland Municipal Airport. The first successful flight from the mainland to Hawaii leaves from Oakland.

1930   Adoption of charter amendments divides Oakland into Council Districts and provides for a council-manager form of government.

1934 Voters approve the East Bay Regional Park District which grows from 10,000 acres of former watershed lands in the East Bay hills to 50,000 acres in Alameda County and 42,000 in Contra Costa County including 59 regional parks and recreation areas, 29 inter-park trails, 10 freshwater swimming areas, two golf courses, and 18 children's play areas.

1935 One of the Depression-era WPA construction projects that help stimulate employment is the construction of the new modern-style Alameda County Courthouse on the shores of Lake Merritt.

1936 The Oakland-San Francisco Bay Bridge, one of the engineering wonders of the world, opens months before the Golden Gate Bridge.

1937 The Broadway low-level tunnel connects Oakland with Contra Costa County. Amelia Earhart begins her ill-fated, around-the-world flight from the Oakland Municipal Airport. In 1997, Linda Finch re-creates Earhart's flight in a restored Lockheed Electra 10E.

1941 Oakland becomes one of the largest points of military manufacturing.

The United States makes a pact with Mexico for workers called braceros to work the fields and later the railroads, for a set amount of time, after which they returned to Mexico. Oakland's Latino population lived, for the most part, in West Oakland during this period.

1942 The Permanente Foundation Hospital is dedicated in Oakland, the first in the chain of Henry J. Kaiser's health plan hospitals.

1942 Paul Robeson sings the national anthem with Oakland dock workers to show support for their labor.

1943 The Pacific Coast leads the nation in shipbuilding. Oakland leads other West Coast cities producing more than 35% of the entire Pacific Coast cargo ship output. Food packing is another major industry with 60% of total food stuffs coming from Oakland canneries.

1946 The Oakland General Strike takes place.

The first Cinco de Mayo event is held in Oakland Auditorium.

1950 Children's Fairyland opens in Lakeside Park. Swelled by huge numbers of workers who flocked to the city for WWII jobs, the U.S. Census puts Oakland's population at 384,575. Oakland's African American population soars from 8,462 in 1940 to 47,562 in 1950. The military makes substantial improvement to the Port's facilities.

1951   Josephine Baker, the famous singer and dancer, leads the fight to get blacks jobs as street car operators in 1951 against Key System Streetcars at the 12th and Broadway headquarters.

1953   The Oakland Board of Education organizes the Oakland Junior College and develops Laney College and Merritt College as separate campuses for the new institution.

1955   Intertribal Friendship House established in Oakland, one of the first urban Indian centers in the country.

1956   Black activists sue to stop the building of the Cypress Freeway; Lionel Wilson, who was subsequently elected mayor, was the attorney.

1962   The first container ships begin arriving in Oakland marking the beginning of dramatic growth of cargo tonnage handled through the Port of Oakland. Fukuoka, Japan becomes Oakland's first sister city.

1964   Construction of Bay Area Rapid Transit (BART) begins. The Port constructs the Seventh Street Marine Terminal, the largest single container terminal on the West Coast.

The Unity Council and the Spanish Speaking Citizens Foundation are both started in the Fruitvale District

Free Speech Movement begins in Berkeley when U.C. administration places a ban on student organizing in Sproul Plaza. Students were organizing against discriminatory hiring practices of Oakland employers, including the *Tribune*, owned by William Knowland.

1965   Bill Russell, who played basketball at McClymonds High School, becomes the first African American NBA coach in the country; 10,000 people march from Berkeley to DeFremery Park, the first anti-war march in California.

1966   Bobby Seale and Huey Newton organize the Black Panther Party for Self-Defense at Oakland City College. The $25.5 million Oakland-Alameda County Coliseum complex opens near I-880.

1969   The Free Breakfast for School Children Program is started at St. Augustine's Church by the Black Panther Party.

Construction on City Center begins with funding provided from matching grants tied to BART construction.

Centro Legal de La Raza founded in the Fruitvale district.

1970 West Oakland native Ron Dellums is elected to Congress, the first African American to be elected from a majority white district.

1972 BART begins operation with its control center above the Lake Merritt station.

The Oakland Athletics Baseball Team wins its first World Championship since relocating from Kansas City.

1974 Asian Health Services is founded in the Chinatown area.

1986 African American business leader Geoffrey Pete becomes the owner of the Athenian/Nile Club, previously a whites-only establishment.

1989 The Loma Prieta earthquake hits the Bay Area collapsing the Cypress Freeway and destroying over 1,000 housing units in Oakland. Forty-five people perish. City Hall suffers structural damage and is evacuated.

1991 Oakland's school board rejects the Houghton Mifflin social studies textbook, which was adopted by the state but opposed by dozens of civil rights and community organizations.

1992 A catastrophic wildfire rages through the Berkeley-Oakland Hills destroying over 3,500 dwellings in Oakland. Twenty-five people perish.

1993 National Oceanic and Atmospheric Administration and Rand McNally rank Oakland's climate the best in the U.S.

1995 Oakland City Hall reopens following an $80 million seismic retrofit and renovation. Fortune ranks California's "Golden Triangle"—Oakland, San Francisco and San Jose—as the #1 place to do business in the U.S.

1996 Oakland's multi-racial school board passes the resolution which has won international praise from linguists for affirming the language rights of African American students (the Ebonics resolution).

1999 Jerry Brown, former State of California governor, is inaugurated as Oakland's 47th mayor.

2002   The African-American Museum and Library opens.

2004   Oakland-based black newspaper, the *Oakland Post* News Group, is purchased by journalist, activist, and former school board member, Paul Cobb.

2006   Former Oakland Congressman Ron Dellums is elected the third African American mayor of Oakland after being recruited to run through a petition campaign.

2010   Oakland begins using ranked-choice voting (also called instant runoff voting).

Jean Quan is elected the first Asian American and first woman mayor of the city of Oakland.

Information in this timeline was obtained from the Oakland History Room of the Oakland Public Library, the Community and Economic Development Agency, and the research of Jaron Kelly Epstein.

References

Ackerman, B. & Alstott, A. (2011, September 20). Tax the wealth. *Los Angeles Times*, p. A11.

Arnold, E. (2010, November 4). Blacks leaving the Bay? New report on black population trends in Oakland reveals 'alarming' results. Retrieved August 1, 2011, from http://oaklandlocal.com/article/blacks-leaving-bay-new-report-black-population-trends-oakland-reveals-'alarming'-results

Aronson, L. (2010, October 15). How they discovered their dream careers: From housekeeper to eco-activist. Retrieved October 29, 2011, fromhttp://www.oprah.com/oprahs-lifeclass/How-Real-Women-Discovered-Their-Dream-Careers/2

Bagdikian, B. (2004). *The new media monopoly*. Boston: Beacon Press. Retrieved from http://books.google.com/books/about/The_new_media_monopoly.html?id=p_VqW4 UMcDMC

Bagwell, B. (1996). *Oakland. The Story of a City*. Oakland Heritage Alliance.

Baker, C. (2007). *Media concentration and democracy: Why ownership matters*. New York: Cambridge University Press. Retrieved from http://books.google.com/books?id=yxA1 Cc8pB3UC&dq=Pippa+Norris&lr=&as_brr=3&ei=aN2sR4m0GIKWzATnlJ2eBg

Baltimoreans react to state takeover plan [Television series episode]. (2006). In city leaders say decision caught them by surprise. Baltimore: WBALtv.

Baxamusa, M. (2008). Empowering communities through deliberation: The model of community benefits agreements. *Journal of Planning Education and Research*, 27, 261. Retrieved May 30, 2011, from http://jpe.sagepub.com/content/27/3/261.abstract

Bell, a.d. (1980). *Brown v. Board of Education* and the interest convergence dilemma. *Harvard Law Review.* Retrieved from http://pscfiles.tamu.edu/links/divcom/bell-interest%20convergence.pdf

Boyd, J. (2009). Union Pacific opens Donner Pass route. *The Journal of Commerce.* Retrieved August 13, 2011, from http://www.joc.com/rail-intermodal/union-pacific-opens-donner-pass-route

Bureau of Labor Statistics, U.S. Department of Labor. Economic News Releases: Table 2 Median weekly earnings of full-time wage and salary workers by union affiliation and selected characteristics. Retrieved September 1, 2011, from http://www.bls.gov/news.rel ease/union2.t02.htm.

Burt, C. (2010, September 14). Opponents say Don Perata trying to buy Oakland mayor's seat. *Oakland Tribune.* Retrieved September 14, 2010, from http://www.notdon.org/bu ying.html

Burt, C, & Rayburn, K. (2008, March 06). Oakland oks industrial land-use policy. *Oakland Tribune.* Retrieved from http://urbanhabitat.org/node/1661

Cammarota, J. & Fine, M. (2008). *Revolutionizing education: Youth participatory action research in motion.* New York: Routledge. Retrieved from http://www.amazon.com-/Revolutionizing-Education-Participatory-Research-Critical/dp/041595616

Cheteji, N. (2010).The racial wealth gap and the borrower's dilemma. *Journal of Black Studies,* 41, 2, 351. Retrieved from http://jbs.sagepub.com/content/41/2/351.short

Clavel, P. (2010). *Activists in City Hall: The progressive response to the Reagan era in Boston and Chicago.* Ithaca, NY: Cornell University Press. Retrieved from http://www.cornellpress.cornell.edu/book/?GCOI=80140100614980

Conley, D. (2001, March). The black-white wealth gap. *The Nation,* 272, 12, 20–22.

Creating crisis: How California teaching policies aggravate racial inequality in public schools. (1999, August). Retrieved August 1, 2011, from http://www.arc.org/content/vi ew/216/36/

Cubberly, E. (1916). Public School Administration. Boston: Houghton-Mifflin.

Davis, R. (1983, April 12). The election of Harold Washington the first black mayor of Chicago. *Chicago Tribune,* p. 1.

Debro, J. (2007, August 1). Confirm Margaret Gordon, champion of environmental justice, to Port Commission. *SF Bay View.* (PAGE?).

Dellums, R., & Halterman, H.L. (2000). *Lying down with the lions: A public life from the streets of Oakland to the halls of power.* Boston: Beacon.

Dempwolf, S. (2010). An evaluation of recent industrial land use studies: Do theory and history matter in practice? Academia.edu. Retrieved August 20, 2011, from http://umcp.academia.edu/ScottDempwolf/Papers/276524/An_Evaluation_of_Recent _Industrial_Land_Use_Studies_Do_Theory_and_History_Matter_In_Practice

Domhoff, G.W. (2005). Power at the local level growth coalition theory. Who Rules America.net. Retrieved August 26, 2011, from http://sociology.ucsc.edu/whorule-samerica/local/growth_coalition_theory.html

Domhoff, G.W. (2009). *Who rules America?* (6ᵗʰ edition) New York: McGraw-Hill.

Doward, J., & Townsend, M. (2009, May 10). G20 police 'used undercover men to incite crowds'. *The Observer*. Retrieved June 10, 2011, from (http://www.guardian.co.uk/politics/2009/may/10/g20-policing-agent-provacateurs)

EBASE. (2007). Retaining manufacturing in Oakland: Exploring land use policy and other strategies for equitable development. Retrieved June 1, 2011, from http://www.bayareavision.org/initiatives/PDFs/Gee_Industrial_Land_Paper_July2007.pdf

Elinson, Z. (2010, September 24). Police, pensions, pot debated by Oakland mayor candidates. *The Bay Citizen*. Retrieved from http://www.baycitizen.org

Elling, D. (2011, April 28). Strong cities, land use policies are key to nation's future. Charles Mott Foundation. Retrieved June 10, 2011, from http://www.mott.org/news/news/2011/20110428CCPKildee.aspx?print=1

Engel, K. (2007). Chamber launches cluster groups. Retrieved August 1, 2011, from http://www.oaklandpartnership.com/news/articles/stories/050207.asp

Epstein, K.A. (2008, September 18). Dellums task force, school district to recruit teachers. *Oakland Post*. (PAGE?)

Epstein, K.K. (2005, Fall).The whitening of the American teaching force: A problem of recruitment or a problem of racism. *Social Justice*, 32, 3, 89–102.

Epstein, K.K (2006). *A different view of urban schools: Civil rights, critical race theory and unexplored realities*. New York: Peter Lang.

Epstein, K.K. (2012). *A different view of urban schools: Civil rights, critical race theory and unexplored realities*. Revised edition New York: Peter Lang.

Fals-Borda, O., & Anisur Rahman, M. (1991). *Action and knowledge: Breaking the monopoly with participatory action research*. New York: Apex.

Feinstein, S. (2010). *The just city*. Ithaca, NY: Cornell University Press.

Ferro, M. (2011, April 28). My word: Developing a coherent five-year plan for public safety. *Oakland Tribune*.

Fetini, A., & Elmusa, K. (2010, November 15). After election, ranked-choice voting gets mixed reviews. *The Bay Citizen*. Retrieved from http://www.baycitizen.org

Gammon, R. (2004, December 8). The man: How Don Perata became the politician he is today. *East Bay Express*. Retrieved from http://www.eastbayexpress.com

Gammon, R. (2007, May 23). Living large; how State Senator Don Perata uses campaign cash to finance his lavish lifestyle. *East Bay Express*. Retrieved from http://www.eastbayexpress.com

Gammon, R. (2010a, February 10). The cancer in the Oakland mayor's race. *East Bay Express*. Retrieved from http://www.eastbayexpress.com

Gammon, R. (2010b, November 7). Jean the giant killer. *East Bay Express*. Retrieved from http://www.eastbayexpress.com

Gammon, R. (2010c, Dec. 15) Crime Dropped Significantly Under Ron Dellums. East Bay Express.

Garcia, K. (2011, April 21). Race for San Francisco mayor lacks any flair. *San Francisco Examiner.* Retrieved from http://www.sfexaminer.com

Gilson, D., & Perot, C. (Designer). (2011). It's the inequality, stupid. [Web Graphic]. Retrieved from http://motherjones.com/politics/2011/02/income-inequality-in-america-chart-graph

Ginwright, S. (2009). *Black youth rising: Activism and radical healing in urban America.* New York: Teachers College Press.

Gonzalez, R. (2005, September 30). Ex-Congressman Dellums may run for mayor. National Public Radio, Retrieved December 3, 2011, from http://www.npr.org/templates/story/story.php?storyId=4930462

Haas, G. (2009, Feb.). Inequality, gentrification, and the right to the city. Peace Works. Retrieved August 24, 2011, from http://www.saje.net/atf/cf/{493B2790DD4E4ED0–8 F4EC78E8F3A7561}/Inequality_And_Gentrification.pdfhttp://www.saje.net/atf/cf/{4 93B2790-DD4E-4ED0–8F4E-C78E8F3A7561}/Inequality_And_Gentrification.pdf

Hammett, C. (1991, January 2). The blind man and the elephant: The explanation of gentrification. *Transactions of the Institute of British Geographers,*16: 173–179.

Hancox, I. (2010, August 25). Re-entry programs help ex-convicts find jobs; repair lives. *Oakland Voices/Oakland Tribune.* Retrieved from http://www.oaklandvoices.us/2010/08 /25/reentry-programs-help-ex-convicts-find-jobs-repair-lives June 20, 2011

Harvey, D. (2009). *Social justice and the city.* Athens: University of Georgia Press.

Hayes, E.C. (1972). *Power structure and urban policy: Who rules in Oakland?* New York: McGraw Hill.

Heredia, C. (2006 June 20). 'We can be a great city' Oakland mayor elect emphasizes citizens' role. *San Francisco Chronicle.*

Heredia, C. (2007a, April 19). Citizen panels urge city to help neighborhoods organize. *San Francisco Chronicle.*

Heredia, C. (2007b, Feb 21). Citizen task forces back community policing as priority. *San Francisco Chronicle.* Retrieved December 1, 2011, from http://articles.sfgate.com/2007–02–21/bay-area/17232427_1_policing-mayor-s-office-officers-union

Heredia, C. (2007c, June 15). Dellums posts results of task force reports. *San Francisco Chronicle.* Retrieved December 1, 2011 from http://articles.sfgate.com/2007–07–15-/bay-area/17252151_1_public-safety-citizen-task-reports

Heredia, C. (2007d March 28). Mayor's panels report on diversity issues. *San Francisco Chronicle,* p.1. Retrieved December 1, 2011, from http://articles.sfgate.com/2007–03–28/bay-area/17235862_1_task-forces-senior-issues-immigration-task

Herr, K., & Anderson, G. (2005). *The action research dissertation: A guide for students and faculty.* Thousand Oaks, CA: Sage.

Id, D. (2009). Oakland city council approves civilianization of citizen OPD complaints. Retrieved from http://www.indybay.org/newsitems/2009/07/08/18606178.php

Info Alameda County (2011, November 28). 2010 Homicide Report. Retrieved Dec. 3 from http://www.infoalamedacounty.org/index.php/Research/Crime-Safety/Homicides/2010-Oakland-Homicide-Report.html

International Trade and Logistics Cluster Update. (2007). Retrieved May 25, 2011, from http://www.oaklandpartnership.com/2008%20Clusters/TL/Trade%20%20Logistics%20Progress%20Report%20as%20of%209%2020%2007.pdf

Jackson, I. (1924). Unpublished master"s thesis. U.C. Berkeley: Berkeley, CA.

Jean Quan becomes first female and Asian American woman elected to Oakland, CA mayorship. (2010, November 11). *Black Christian News.* Retrieved June 15, 2011 from http://blackchristiannews.com

Jennings, J. (2010). The state of Black Boston:.Blackstonian the black Boston. Retrieved from http://blackstonian.com/news/wp-content/uploads/2011/06/stateofblackboston-jennings.pdf

Johnson, C. (2009, May 29). With probe over, Perata primed to lead Oakland. *San Francisco Chronicle.* Retrieved from http://articles.sfgate.com/2009–05–29/bay-area/17201087_1_sen-don-perata-oakland-voters-federal-probe

Jones, F. (2006, May 28). New and old strategies in the race for mayor of Oakland. *Gibbs Magazine,* Retrieved from http://www.gibbsmagazine.com/A%20New%20Campaign%20Strategy%20in%20Oakland.htm

Kennedy, M. & Tilly, C. (1990). Transformative populism and the development of a community of color. In Kling, J.M., & Posner, P.S., *Dilemmas of activism: Class, community, and the politics of local mobilization.* Philadelphia: Temple University Press.

Kerr, D. (2010, July 16). An anarchist gives his take on Mehserle protest freedom fighters. *Oakland Local.*

Kochhar, R., Fry, R. & Taylor, P. (2011). Wealth gaps rise to record highs between whites, blacks, Hispanics. Pew Research Center. Retrieved July 26, 2011, from http://pewsocialtrends.org/2011/07/26/wealth-gaps-rise-to-record-highs-between-whites-blacks-hispanics/8/#chapter-7-trends-in-household-wealth-1984-to-2009

Kuruvila, M. (2010a, October 16). Oakland mayoral foes trying to stop Don Perata. *San Francisco Chronicle.* Retrieved from http://articles.sfgate.com/2010–10–16/bay-area/24138149_1_greg-harland-voting-system-joe-tuman

Kuruvila, M. (2010b, November 11). Jean Quan wins Oakland mayor's race. *San Francisco Chronicle.* Retrieved from http://articles.sfgate.com/2010–11–11/news/24826082_1_-ranked-choice-voting-second-and-third-choice-second-and-third-place-votes

Kuruvila, M. (2010c, November 6). Jean Quan takes Oakland lead from Don Perata. *San Francisco Chronicle.* Retrieved from http://articles.sfgate.com/2010–11–06/news/24817658_1_ranked-choice-voting-second-and-third-place-votes-instant-runoffs

Kuruvila, M. (2010d, November 12). Don Perata concedes Oakland mayor's race to Quan. *San Francisco Chronicle.* Retrieved from http://articles.sfgate.com/2010–11–12/news/24828113_1_ranked-choice-voting-mayoral-election-election-day

Lehrer, J. (2010, December 17). "A Physicist Solves the City." *New York Times Magazine*. Retrieved December 3, 2011, from http://www.nytimes.com/2010/12/19/magazine/19Urban_West-t.html?pagewanted=all

Logan, J., & Swanstrom, T. (1990). *Beyond the city limits: Urban policy and economic restructuring in comparative perspective*. Philadelphia: Temple University Press.

Maher, S. (2011a, June 12). Oakland considering using civilians to investigate police complaints. *Oakland Tribune*. Retrieved December 1, 2011, from http://www.insidebayarea.com/top-stories/ci_18260072

Maher, S. (2011b, September 21). Oakland police under new scrutiny by judge who threatened federal takeover. *San Jose Mercury News*. Retrieved December 1, 2011, from http://www.mercurynews.com/breaking-news/ci_18947723

Marcuse, P., Connolly, J., Novy, J., Olivo, I., Potter, C. and Steil, J. (2009). *Searching for the just city: Debates in urban theory and practice*. New York: Routledge.

Maritime first: APL 'cold-irons' ships in Oakland to clear the air, a. (2011, June 04). Retrieved June 4, 2011, from http://wavesnewsletter.com/?p=2654

Maryland port commissioners. (2011). Retrieved August 6, 2011, from http://www.mpa.maryland.gov/content/MPA-Divisions-port-commissioners.php

Matier, P., & Ross, A. (2006, June 19). Dellums victory signifies a sea change in Oakland politics. *San Francisco Chronicle*. Retrieved from http://www.sfgate.com/cgi-bin/article.cgi?f=/c/a/2006/06/19/BAG8QJGCDN1.DTL#ixzz1OjQrnzlp

Mayfield, K. (2007, Jan 4). Grassroots democracy sprouts in Oakland. *San Francisco Chronicle*. Retrieved December 1, 2011 from http://articles.sfgate.com/2007-01-04/opinion/17226127_1_task-force-ron-dellums-mayoral

Mayfield, K. (2010, November 01). Mayor's task forces achieve policies that slow gentrification. *Oakland Local*. Retrieved June 20, 2011, from http://oaklandlocal.com/blogs/2010/10/mayor's-task-forces-achieve-policies-slow-gentrification-community-voices

Mayor Dellums presents industrial land use policy to city council. (2008, March 3). US Fed News Service, including US State News. Retrieved June 18, 2011, from General Interest Module. (Document ID: 1465512541)

McIntyre, A. (2007). *Participatory Action Research*. Thousand Oaks, CA: Sage.

McNair, D. (2011, March 29). Into the breach. Retrieved from http://communityrenewal.ca/i4gateway004-breach

Media Access Project. [Web log message]. (2011). Retrieved from http://www.mediaaccess.org/issues/media-concentration/

Mitchell, D. (2003). *The right to the city: Social justice and the fight for public space*. New York: Guilford.

Molotch, H. (1976). The city as a growth machine: Toward a political economy of place. *American Journal of Sociology*, 82, 2: 309–332.

Molotch, H. (1990). Urban deals in comparative perspective. In Logan, J., and Swanstrom, T., *Beyond the City Limits: Urban policy and economic restructuring in comparaative perspective*. Philadelphia: Temple University Press, pp. 175–198.

Molotch, H. (2007). Growth machine links: Up, down and across. In Jonas, A., and Wilson, D. *The urban growth machine: Critical perspectives, two decades later*, pp. 175–193.

Motlach, J. (2011, Nov. 3) How Occupy Oakland Is Stealing Occupy Wall Street's Mojo. *Time Magazine* http://www.time.com/time/nation/article/0,8599,2098628,00.html

Mullane, N. (2010). Port of Oakland redevelopment has potential to revive Oakland [Radio series episode]. In Mullane, N. (executive producer), *Crosscurrents*. Oakland: KALW News.

Murphy, K. (2009, January 22). Oakland's teacher turnover problem. The Education Report. Retrieved September 15, 2011, from http://www.ibabuzz.com/education/2009/01/22/oaklands-teacher-turnover-problem/

Muwakkil, S. (2006, June 20). Black politics paradigm paradox. *In These Times* newspaper.

Neidhardt, L. (2009, April 7). Mayor Dellums deserves your respect. *San Francisco Chronicle*.

Newhouse, D. (2010, October 18). Four mayor hopefuls on the hot seat. *Oakland Tribune*. Retrieved from http://www.insidebayarea.com/

Norton, M. (2011, May 20). Living beyond your means. *New York Times*. Retrieved November 20, 2011, from http://www.nytimes.com/roomfordebate/2011/03/21-/rising-wealth-inequality-should-we-care/living-beyond-your-means-when-youre-not-rich

Oak to Ninth CBA. (2006). The partnership for working families. Retrieved August 30, 2011, from http://www.communitybenefits.org/article.php?id=1467.

Oakland, be a good citizen in the fight for health [Web log message]. (2010, November 07). Retrieved from http://public inc.blogspot.com/2010_11_07_archive.html

Oakland dance form goes global with viral clips. (2011, May 27) KTVU (2009).

Oakland mayor Ron Dellums tries to calm crowd. (2009). [Print Photo]. Retrieved from http://www.flickr.com/photos/thomashawk/3179331172/in/photostream/

Oakland partnership two-year report. (2009). [Web Graphic]. Retrieved July 26, 2011, from http://www.oaklandpartnership.com/2008%20Quick%20Links/Reports/Reports.htm

Perkins, D. (2011, July 21). Culture clash: Race and class conflict in a neighborhood engineered to bridge society's gaps. *Alexandria Times*, p. 1

Personal Interview with Margaret Gordon. (June 2010).

Pew Hispanic Center. (2009). Demographic profile of Hispanics in California, 2009. Retrieved from http://pewhispanic.org/states/?stateid=CA

Pew Insight Center. (2010). Closing the racial wealth gap initiative. Retrieved Feb. 2, 2011, from http://www.insightcced.org/communities/Closing-RWG.html

Police accused of using provocateurs at summit [Television series episode]. (2007). Toronto: Toronto Star.

Port of Oakland. (2009). A market first as Port of Oakland breaks new ground in US port terminal concession agreements [Press release]. Retrieved from http://www.portofoakland.com/newsroom/pressrel/view.asp?id=16

Port of Oakland. (2010). Northern California mega region summit moving America's economic recovery forward. [Press release]. Retrieved from http://www.portofoakland.com/newsroom/pressrel/view.asp?id=197

Port of Oakland officials. (2011). Retrieved August 15, 2011, from http://www.portofoakland.com/portnyou/offi_comm.asp

Profile: Antanas Mockus. (2010). Colombia reports. Retrieved October 1, 2011, from http://colombiareports.com/colombia-news/149–2010-elections/9185-profile-antanas-mockus.html

Public divided on Occupy Wall Street Protesters. (2011, Oct. 5). Rasmussen Reports. Retrieved October 27, 2011, from http://www.rasmussenreports.com/public_content/business/federal_bailout/october_2011/public_divided_on_occupy_wall_street_protesters

Purcell, M. (2008). *Recapturing democracy: Neoliberalization and the struggle for alternative urban futures.* New York: Routledge.

Ranghelli, L. (2011). Building the progressive city. *Shelterforce The Journal of Affordable Housing and Community Building,* Retrieved from http://www.shelterforce.org/article/2118/building_the_progressive_city/August

Reich, R. (2011, Feb. 15). Why we should raise taxes on the super rich and lower them on the middle class. *Huffington Post.*

Rhomberg, C. (1998).White nativism and urban politics: The 1920s Ku Klux Klan in Oakland, California. *Journal of American Ethnic History* 17/2:39–55.

Richman, J. (2010, November 11). Inside Don Perata's mayoral election defeat. *Oakland Tribune.* Retrieved from http://www.ibabuzz.com/politics/2010/11/11/inside-don-peratas-mayoral-election-defeat/

Roobs. (2011, August 06). Playing with politics: A blog on law, politics, planning, development, and other vices [Web log message]. Retrieved from http://playingwithpolitics.wordpress.com/2011/08/06/missing-the-forrest-because-of-the-trees-gentrification/#more-1079

Ryan, A. (2010). Education for the people: The Third World student movement at San Francisco State College and City College of New York. Ohio State University Dissertation. Retrieved October 1, 2010, from http://etd.ohiolink.edu/view.cgi/Ryan%20Angela%20Rose.pdf?osu1275416332

Ryan, L. (2011, July 1). Holy Names University expands access. *Oakland Tribune.*

Schemo, D. (2006, March 30). Maryland acts to take over failing Baltimore schools. *The New York Times.* Retrieved from http://www.nytimes.com/2006/03/30/education/30child.htm

Schrag, P. (2004). *Paradise lost: California's experience, America's future.* Berkeley: University of California Press.

Shapiro, T., Meschede, T., & Sullivan, L. (2010). *The racial wealth gap increases four fold.* Research and Policy Brief Institute. Institute on Assets and Social Policy. Brandeis University.

Sinclair, U. (1924). *The Goslings.* Pasadena, California: The state of the city: 2007–2011. Retrieved August 30, 2011, from http://www.scribd.com/doc/43153042/Oak-023443

Tan, C. (2010, May 6). Hispanics' unemployment rate soars. *Los Angeles Times.*

Taylor, J. (2010, December 21). Jesse Allen-Taylor's pen punk'dPerata. *The Oakland Post.* Retrieved from http://content.postnewsgroup.com/?p=10683

Taylor, J. (2008, March 27). *Berkeley Daily Planet.*

Terman, L. (1916). *The measurement of intelligence.* New York: Houghton Mifflin.

Tyack, D. (1974). *The one best system.* Cambridge, MA: Harvard University Press.

Urban Strategies Council. (2011, Nov. 28). 2010 Oakland Homicide Report, Retrieved Dec. 2, 2011, from http://www.infoalamedacounty.org/index.php/Research/Crime-Safety/Homicides/2010-Oakland-Homicide-Report.html

U.S. Senate. (1976, April 23). Supplementary detailed staff reports or intelligence activities and the rights of Americans, Book Iii, *Final report of the select committee to study governmental operations with respect to intelligence activities.*

Voyles, S.(2010, Jan. 5). Union Pacific alters tunnels for double-stacked trains. *Reno Gazette-Journal,* p. 1.

Wagstaff, E. (2010, September 15). Oakland mayoral candidates protest Perata spending. *Oakland North.* Retrieved July 12, 2011 from http://oaklandnorth.net/2010/09/15-/oakland-mayoral-candidates-protest-perata-spending/

Weinstein, J. (1962). Organized business and the commission and manager movements. *Journal of Southern History* 28:166–182.

Wilkerson, I. (2011). *The warmth of other suns.* New York: Vintage.

Wilson D., Wouters J., Grammenos, D. (2004). Successful protect-community discourse: Spatiality and politics in Chicago's Pilsen neighborhood. *Environment and Planning* 36(7): 1173–1190.

Yang, K.W. (2009 Fall). Mathematics, critical literacy, and youth participatory action research. *New Directions in Youth Development.* 123:99–118.

Zamora, J. (2007, March 10). Architeckz look to build outlet for Oakland youth; Dance troupe channels emotions through 'turf dancing,' a younger sibling of 1980s break dancing. *San Francisco Chronicle.*

Index